ISRAELI POETRY

JEWISH LITERATURE AND CULTURE

Series Editor, Alvin H. Rosenfeld

ISRAELI POETRY

A CONTEMPORARY ANTHOLOGY

Selected and Translated by

Warren Bargad & Stanley F. Chyet

INDIANA UNIVERSITY PRESS   BLOOMINGTON AND INDIANAPOLIS

First Midland Book Edition 1988

Versions of a number of these translations appeared in *Ammi, Jerusalem
Quarterly, Midstream, P.E.N. Israel 1974, Shirim,* and *TriQuarterly.*

Manufactured in the United States of America

Library of Congress Cataloging in Publication Data
Main entry under title:

Israeli poetry.

(Jewish literature and culture)
Bibliography: p.
Includes index.
1. Israeli poetry—Translations into English.
2. English poetry—Translations from Hebrew.
I. Bargad, Warren. II. Chyet, Stanley F. III. Series.
PJ5059.E3187 1985   892.4'16'08   84-48247
(cl.) ISBN 0-253-33140-4
(pa.) ISBN 0-253-20356-2

2 3 4 5 6 92 91 90 89 88

To Arlene, Rob, and Adena
and
To Geri, Michael, and Susan

CONTENTS

ISRAELI POETRY

INTRODUCTION

Israeli poetry? To earlier generations the prospect of *any* sort of Israeli literature would have seemed extraordinary, chimerical, even miraculous. A famous visitor to Ottoman Palestine in the 1860s—Mark Twain—found there a land that sat "in sackcloth and ashes," a land "desolate and unlovely"; Jerusalem herself was "become a pauper village," "mournful, and dreary, and lifeless"; all around her was "dismal scenery . . . a hopeless, dreary heartbroken land." If the land was "sacred to poetry and tradition,"[1] it was beyond imagining that *new* poetry could be produced there.

Before we turn to that poetry, it will be helpful to contemplate tradition and to distinguish Israeli literature (which Twain's generation could not have anticipated) from a larger, much older literary phenomenon, Hebrew literature (of which he and his contemporaries surely had some awareness).[2] It ought to be kept in mind, as we consider what Israeli poets have achieved in recent decades, that there has been no time since the biblical period began—that is, no time in the past four thousand years—when Hebrew has not been put to literary use. Until this century, of course, Hebrew literary productivity almost invariably reflected Jewish religious commitments, not secular values. Whether the literary expression was poetry or history or liturgy or law or philosophy, it was bound to be a religious, and not at all a secular, instrument—if only because before the French Revolution and the ensuing wave of modernism, no sharp line could be drawn between the secular and the religious in Jewish experience; both were thoroughly interwoven in an entire way of living and of looking at the world.

In any case, Hebrew was never a dead language, never a forgotten or an abandoned idiom. On the contrary, it was the thread that ran through all of Jewish history. It was inevitably a major foundation of Jewish identity precisely because the Jewish community had never allowed it to die. That is why, when a century and a half ago Jews came into substantial contact with the socioeconomic, political, and cultural forms characteristic of Western and Central Europe and had to adapt themselves to the evolution of a confusing modern world, Hebrew could serve them as a sort of natural moralizing force. Everyone with a modicum of Jewish education had some access to it, though only the intellectual elite ever really mastered it. Still, in theory at least, all Jews had in common the heritage of the Hebrew language and its literature. If ideas of a revived national life for the Jews were to prove valid, Hebrew would have to be recognized as central to the enterprise; though less than a vernacular, it would have to play something of the role that Italian—the *lingua toscana*—played in the Risorgimento, and German—*Hochdeutsch*—in the eventual, if short-lived, unification of the Kaiserreich.

Hebrew, after all, could claim tremendous prestige, not only among Jews who regarded it as a bridge between past and future glories (and what is valued more than "glories" in the psychic economy of an emergent national liberation movement?), but also among non-Jews, even unfriendly non-Jews, since both Christianity and Islam owe so much to biblical Judaism and have been compelled to regard Hebrew antiquity as a source for their own spiritual aspirations. Hebrew, then, gave Jews a certain status, however grudging it may have been, in Christian and even in Moslem eyes, because neither Christianity nor Islam was conceivable without the biblical—that is, the Hebrew—past. Hebrew in consequence contributed markedly to Jewish self-esteem. All these factors were influential during the past hundred years, when Jews in Europe began creating a modern literature of their own. A key though never an exclusive role was naturally enough assigned Hebrew as this new Jewish literature took shape to express the changes overtaking Jewish life and to mitigate European resistance to the hope of Jewish equality.

The Hebrew literary effort in the Diaspora always involved a struggle, often one surpassingly bitter and complex. On the one hand, even when Jews confronted secular modernity, the religious norms that had for so long been virtually identical with Hebrew literary expression could not be set aside entirely. On the other hand, modernist Jews who prized their Jewish identity and wanted Jewish distinctiveness to survive found it necessary to develop something Hebrew had not known to any significant degree—not for centuries at any rate—belles lettres, a literary product that could address the changes increasingly visible on the Jewish street and could accommodate European secular modernity rather than expend its energies mainly on questions of religious concern. This effort could not be "organic" in the way it was organic for writers in English or French or German or Russian, languages all widely spoken as well as written by large populations and not the special property of intellectual or cultural elites. Hebrew's role as a vernacular—if any—was very limited, and the language had to struggle fiercely for the right to reflect Jewish experience in the modern world. The creators of modern Hebrew had to pit themselves against determined opposition to the modernization of Hebrew and against the charge that they were dismissing religion and courting heresy. In addition, they had to contend with the greater popularity of other Jewish languages—most notably Yiddish, of course, but in the Mediterranean, Ladino or Judeo-Arabic—and they had to struggle against the languages of the non-Jewish peoples in whose midst Jews lived and with whose social and cultural institutions Jews wanted to amalgamate. In any case, it was only in 1890 that Eliezer Ben-Yehuda's Hebrew Language Council was organized and only in 1910 that his monumental *Complete Dictionary of Ancient and Modern Hebrew* began appearing.

Israeli literature is, of course, not identical with Hebrew literature. Israeli literature, that body of writing produced in *Erets Yisrael*, the Land of Israel, and ultimately, after 1948, in *Medinat Yisrael*, the State of Israel, is on the whole a much more organic growth than the modern Hebrew literature created during the past century outside the Promised Land. Israeli literature, after all, has emerged from and reflects the experience of a sizable population, one that speaks as well as reads and writes Hebrew. In that sense, Israeli literature is a much less exotic, much less eccentric phenomenon than the Hebrew literature written in the Ukraine or Southern Poland or Paris or Berlin or New York. Israeli literature is not at utter odds with its environment and need fear no serious linguistic competitors.

The Zionist achievement, notwithstanding its defects and imperfections, is a tremendous one. No national revival in the world exceeds it in intensity, drama, and self-realization, or in the level of its cultural expression—and that achievement, whatever else it is, is a Hebrew achievement. Hebrew, in short, is identified with a remarkably bold and successful enterprise, the reconstitution of Jewish national life and sovereignty in the promised land of Jewish history. Its success gives Hebrew, Israeli Hebrew, great élan and energy but also poses problems whose proportions are not inconsiderable.

Israel is geographically part of the Middle East—and indeed is a major factor in contemporary Middle Eastern consciousness. Yet as astute an Israeli intellectual as Shulamit Hareven defines literary Israel as a territory whose borders skirt present-day Manhattan and nineteenth-century Odessa, with Czernowitz somewhere in between. She would prefer a more Mediterranean Israel, though she surely knows that such an Israel is, in literary as well as political terms, still very much within the realm of utopian fantasy.[3] Yoram Bronowski, too, is clear on this point: that Israeli literature moves willy-nilly on paths determined by European literature.[4] It does seem that, for literary purposes, the Israeli sensibility is incontrovertibly a Euro-American sensibility. Very little about Israeli belles lettres can be called Levantine, even though a sizable proportion of the Israeli population (a segment that includes such authors as A. B. Yehoshua, Nissim Aloni, and Erez Bitoun) has Levantine or Oriental antecedents. From a Middle Eastern perspective, then, all Israelis, even those of Moroccan or Persian or Yemenite origin, are European; their literature is European; their outlook is alien or external to the Middle East. This detachment from the Levant is both a blessing and a curse. It is surely related to the morbidity that Natan Zach detects in so much Israeli fiction[5] (though, as Leslie Fiedler could testify,[6] the Israelis do not hold a monopoly on this tendency). Another, related aspect of Israel's Europeanism is the consciousness of the Holocaust that weighs so heavily on the Israeli psyche. It may be said without hesitation that for a great many Israelis, the Holocaust is the immovable emotional reality. The smoke of Auschwitz has yet to vanish from the skies over Jerusalem and Tel Aviv.

Another problem: Israel, the Hebrew-speaking, Hebrew-writing, Hebrew-reading society of contemporary Israel, is in the main expressive of secular tendencies, indeed is a society scarcely less secular or consumerist than any other in the Western industrialized world. Even so, the past, in which religion and secular activity were mostly undivided, in which the quotidian was regulated by pietist norms, has not vanished. At the very least psychologically—and often politically—it remains on the scene and in force. That circumstance means (or has meant thus far) that there is a religious dimension to every Israeli governing coalition, even the most anticlerical, and for writers it means that Hebrew today in Israel is—in ways that are not necessarily obvious—as much the language of an embattled society as it ever was in Europe. For Israeli society is embattled tout court: not just externally, vis-à-vis its neighbors to the east and the north, but internally as well, caught in daily confrontations between tradition and modernity, agrarianism and industrialism, socialism and capitalism, Judaism experienced historically as a religious civilization and Judaism experienced as modern secular statehood.

Israelis, and especially the writers in their midst, have never had an opportunity to relax. The situation of facing a past that is always visible, always felt, with all its tensions, all its abrasions and dislocations, is not unique to the Hebrew language or to Israeli society. Still, it would seem legitimate to argue that the pressures on that society are uncommonly severe and, of course, very much complicated by the conditions of Jewish life and history in recent decades: the glare and stink of the Holocaust, an ongoing state of war with the Arab League, and the exertion of absorbing a million newcomers in scarcely more than a generation—absorbing them linguistically as well as socially and economically, in itself an immense, daunting challenge. But in fact, all of Jewish history, the farflung Jewish dispersion, clamors to be heard, recognized, pondered, brooded over. Israeli writers can never be free of an inner turmoil, an inner restlessness, possibly even a certain guilt, which, one supposes, writers in other societies encounter, if at all, to a far lesser degree. To be sure, this condition of conflict in which Israeli writers find themselves is not without its distinct advantages; the poet Anadad Eldan has put it very well: No work of art is given birth by tranquility.

A secular, belletristic literature, we have said, is not a well-established Hebrew tradition. Israeli writers, in creating an innovative literary product in Hebrew, have had to wrestle with the "personality" Hebrew developed during most of its lengthy progress from biblical antiquity to the twentieth century. Undoubtedly there is something liberating in that act of creation, but it is accompanied by a certain measure of conflict. We must remember that writers using Hebrew have until recent generations typically expressed themselves as members of a collectivity, one that saw itself and was even seen by others as *am segula*, a God-chosen community. Israeli writers, as modern writers, have been forced to focus on individualistic, even private sensibilities. They have had to confront themselves as individuals, but what might properly be called the numinous past, the sacred history of the Jews, has not lost its potency altogether. Therefore, they experience a kind of tension unknown to writers whose language has no grandiose religio-national past or tradition to assert a claim on them. Ludwig Lewisohn saw a work of art as "life projected and interpreted by a significant personality" and believed that modern literature was tantamount to "moral research, a road to salvation."[7] But these are not norms sanctified by Hebrew literary history. One ought not underestimate the possible psychic hazards, the atavistic sense of perpetrating a betrayal—of going against, setting aside patterns, a mind set, dating back twenty-five or thirty centuries. Even their liberation can be for Israeli writers an abiding source of anxiety.

Israeli poetry. Clearly its roots go back far beyond 1948, the year the State of Israel was founded. Its roots are to be found, in part, in the literary developments of the 1920s and 1930s, the decades that saw the Yishuv, the Jewish population of Palestine, evolve socially, culturally, and politically in conformity with the ideology of aliya and *hagshama*—the Zionist ideals of settling in the Land of Israel and realizing the dream of Jewish national rebirth. But certainly the roots go deeper, to the turn of the century, to the modern, European-born classics of Hebrew poetry, to Chaim Nachman Bialik and Saul Tchernichovsky.

While the early Zionist congresses debated the political practicalities and ideological and cultural foundations of Jewish nationalism—and, in 1906, declared Hebrew the "national language" of the Jewish people—Bialik (1873–1934) was writing poems on the crisis of modernity in Jewish culture, on the traumatic disruption of traditional Judaism by the culturally reformist Haskalah (Enlightenment) and by the nascent nationalist movement itself. Tchernichovsky (1875–1943) celebrated, rather than bemoaned, the onset of modernity by producing Hebrew verse in an abundance of modern poetic genres: sonnets and sonnet cycles, narrative poems, ballads, nature lyrics, odes, and more. Bialik's poetry expressed the transition; Tchernichovsky's confirmed it. Both were the markers of modernity in the Hebrew poetic tradition.

The tradition of modern Hebrew poetry goes back further, to its European beginnings in the late eighteenth century. The founders of the tradition are generally identified as the scholars and writers, experts in the Hebrew language and knowledgeable in German, who assisted the philosopher Moses Mendelssohn (1729–86) with his translation of the Hebrew Bible into German (1782). The first Hebrew journal, *haMe'asef* (Gleaner or Anthology), was founded at Koenigsberg, Prussia, in 1783. The cover of the third issue featured the likeness of Naftali Herz Wessely (1725–1805), a reformist educator and author who was the acknowledged leader of the Hebrew literary movement (later dubbed the Haskalah). Beginning in 1789, Wessely penned a cycle of poems on the heroic figure of Moses called *Shirei Tif'eret* (Songs of glory).

Much of Haskalah poetry (and drama in verse) published through the 1860s was written, as was *Shirei Tif'eret*, in high biblical diction, clearly in imitation of the German neoclassical style. (A notable exception was M. Y. Lebensohn's *Shirei Bat Tsiyon* [Songs of the daughter of Zion, Vilna, 1841], a collection of lyric poetry.) The main thrust of these writings was the Haskalah perception of poetry as a medium of social and cultural change, an educational tool for the advancement of religious reform, acculturation, and Jewish ethical humanism. The epitome of this didactic art was the poetry of Yehuda Leib Gordon (1830–92) of Vilna, whose programmatic poem "Hakitsa, ami" (Awake, my people) and other, longer narrative works urged acceptance of the Enlightenment's antitraditional values.

The assassination of the comparatively liberal Czar Alexander II in 1881 and the subsequent repression of and pogroms against the Jews of Russia put an abrupt end to the Haskalah's idealized notions of acculturation and emancipation. Leo Pinsker's (1821–91) idea of "auto [i.e., self]-emancipation" and the gradually strengthening idea of a Jewish return to the Land of Israel began to come to the fore. The "Hovevei Tsiyon" (Lovers of Zion) movement grew increasingly active in the 1880s, and the first large group of Jewish colonists (the so-called Bilu aliya) left Russia for Palestine in 1881–82 and eventually established the villages of Rishon Letsiyon and Zikhron Ya'akov. A popular poet of the period was M. M. Dolitsky (1850–1931), whose works, though perhaps not a great artistic achievement, spread the word of Hovevei Tsiyon. But the more significant response, in the 1890s, was a grand debate in the flourishing Hebrew press on the whole concept—and possibility—of Jewish nationhood. At the same time came the great Hebrew poetic "renaissance," centered on the figures of Bialik and Tchernichovsky.

Bialik, having left the renowned Volozhin yeshiva at the age of seventeen, came to Odessa in 1891. Odessa was a center of literary activity, both Yiddish and Hebrew: Mendele Mokher Seforim (S. Y. Abramovitz,

1835–1917), Ahad Ha'am (Asher Ginsberg, 1856–1927), Moshe Leib Lilienblum (1843–1910), Peretz Smolenskin (1842–85), M. Y. Berditchevsky (1865–1921), Sholom Aleichem (Shalom Rabinovitz, 1859–1916), and Tchernichovsky were among the writers who lived and worked there in this period. It was the famous publicist Ahad Ha'am, editor of the important periodical *haShilo'aḥ*, who became Bialik's mentor. Ahad Ha'am's essays stressed the organic nature of Judaism and the spiritual and cultural continuity of the Jewish people as it proceeded to develop a modern, national consciousness. While Jews moved toward secular nationhood, the central values and teachings of Judaism—impartial justice and rationalism, in Ahad Ha'am's thinking—had to be preserved. Bialik's poetry is both a paean to and a eulogy for the world of traditional Judaism. For decades his works were also interpreted as an expression of modern Jewish national rebirth. Tchernichovsky's works were more daring: he openly challenged traditional frameworks and beliefs by writing about Canaanite gods, Hellenistic devotion to beauty, and the universal love of nature. Between these two poets and their dichotomous messages of trauma and renewal, Hebrew poetry at the turn of the century offered an anguished yet exhilarating perspective of the Jewish people on the threshold of a new, uncertain existence.

The Russian Revolution and the subsequent establishment of the Soviet Union spelled disaster for Hebrew culture in Russia. All Hebrew presses and publications were completely shut down. The Enlightenment came to an abrupt end. In 1921 Bialik and Tchernichovsky, along with most other Hebrew writers, emigrated from Russia; later, after spending some years in Berlin, both came to Tel Aviv, Bialik in 1924 and Tchernichovsky in 1931. The "Third Aliya," the aliya of the *ḥalutsim*, the "pioneers," was on.

During the twenties and early thirties the younger poets of this aliya— Uri Zvi Greenberg (1894–1981), Avraham Shlonsky (1900–1973), and Natan Alterman (1910–70)—came to dominate the Yishuv's cultural scene. Shlonsky's background was rooted in Hasidism, Zionism, socialism, and Russian revolutionary poetry. After turning to physical labor and spending a year at the Sorbonne, Shlonsky eventually gathered around him a group of young writers, founded new literary journals, and, in the late thirties, established Sifriat Poalim (The Workers' Library), which remains one of Israel's major literary publishing houses. Bialik's heir apparent—poet, editor, essayist, publisher, cultural guru, linguistic innovator, translator, promoter of young talent—Shlonsky moved assertively in 1931 to exorcise Bialik and his works as outdated, inflexible, too conservative artistically and linguistically. (Bialik, in turn, attacked the new poetry as too radical and discontinuous with the tradition.) With Bialik's death in 1934, Shlonsky became the undisputed leader of the lit-

erary establishment and remained in this position for the next thirty
years.

The other predominant force in Hebrew poetry from the thirties to the
sixties was Shlonsky's younger contemporary, Natan Alterman. Arriving
in Israel at age fifteen in 1925, Alterman studied at the renowned Herzliya
gymnasium in Tel Aviv and then spent several years at Nancy, France,
completing his degree in agronomy. Poetry, however, became his vocation.
He burst upon the literary scene with tremendous force with his early
works *Kokhavim Baḥuts* (Stars outside, 1938) and the immensely popu-
lar *Simḥat Aniyim* (Joy of the poor, 1941). Through the mid-1960s Alter-
man was a complete presence: the droll political humor in his satirical
"haTur haShevi'i" (Seventh column) poems in the weekly press captivated
Israeli readers throughout the 1940s; his witty cabaret lyrics and his
translations of Shakespeare, Russian and French poetry, even *Winnie the
Pooh*, and, later, his own plays, provided continual entertainment. A
whole generation of young, talented poets sat at his feet in the literary
cafés of Tel Aviv. It was, however, the newness of his poetry, with its am-
biguous, French-inspired symbolism, its haunting, balladic style, and its
clever rhyming patterns, that made Alterman the looming figure in the
world of Israeli poetry nearly until his death.

This poetic giant was ultimately challenged by the Berlin-born Natan
Zach (1930–   ). Beginning in the late 1950s, Zach set about liberat-
ing Israeli poetry from what he considered to be a fixed, monotonous,
Altermanian style. His main argument was that Alterman's works were
too mannered, too stylized; he accused Alterman of elevating regular
meter, rhyme, and symmetry over the fundamental semantic unit, the
sentence. It seemed to Zach, in other words, that the primary goal of
Alterman's poetry was structure, not any logical statement of meaning.
Whatever the truth of these arguments, Zach's aim clearly was to en-
gender a complete literary reassessment, an effort that culminated in his
1966 work *Zman Veritmus etsel Bergson Uvashira haModernit* (Time
and rhythm in Bergson and in modern poetry). More than a personal
diatribe, Zach's attempt reflected a much broader shift in poetic taste and
influence: a moving away from Russian structures and symbolist imagery
toward the less formal, more colloquial style of modern British and
American poetry.

During the 1950s Israel herself, in fact, politically and culturally, was
moving away from her East European–Russian roots toward a Western
sphere of influence. Zach's rebellion actually represents the climax of a
growing search for identity among the younger Israeli poets. In 1953 the
manifesto of the journal *Likrat* (Toward) stated that it opposed the "holy
enthusiasm" of the War of Independence generation, because the writers
of that group "had not met the strict test of secularity." The goal of the

new generation was "toward no direction except that of the individual [artistic] development of each one of us." A purported group psychology and group values were to be replaced by individualistic varieties of creative writing. The younger Israeli poets of the 1950s and 1960s were seeking not only the new poetic style that Zach advocated but also the possibilities of a poetry unencumbered by cultural influence. Their ideal was a poetry natural—not highly allusive—in its language and open in its topics to the whole gamut of human experience.

While not in essence new—Shlonsky and Bialik themselves had been purposeful innovators, and the entire subject of tradition and change had been heatedly debated since the 1890s—the individualistic trend in Israeli poetry has gained increasing strength in the last thirty years. Despite the oft-stated (and by now old-hat) critique, "Where are they going?" (*le'an hem holkhim*),[8] Israeli poets have persisted in understanding poetry as a pluralistic venture, a means of personal artistic statement.

The collection of poetry made available in this volume spans approximately the last forty years of Hebrew poetic activity. Certainly not *all* Israeli poets, not even all *great* Israeli poets, could be represented. The selection of eleven poets was based mainly on the aim of offering the reader a group of poets who would be representative of Israeli poetry in its artistic achievement, its varied styles, and its literary history. A second fundamental choice was also made: to limit the number of poets in order to include a greater number of poems by each one. In this way the reader would have a broader exposure to each writer than is usually possible with anthologies, and would thereby come to know well a number of individual personalities.

In selecting the poems for translation, a certain subjectivity and a number of technical considerations were operative. Having read through all the poets' published collections, the translators chose the poems they found most engaging. However, the selection process was also governed by an awareness of the needs of a generally uninitiated audience. Technical considerations were, from the beginning, primary. In most instances poems with regular rhyming patterns were avoided; the translators felt that they could not do them justice, that the translations might reduce the poetry to kitsch. At the same time, it was clear that the vast majority of poems produced by Israeli poets have been written in free verse, so that the anthology does indeed reflect this contemporary trend.

Other guidelines have been followed in compiling this collection: a feeling for individual artistic development, and a sense of history. First, poems have been selected from nearly every published collection of each poet; and these poems are presented in chronological order within the sections devoted to the respective poets. In this manner the translators wish to stimulate an awareness of the creative developments and changes experienced by each poet. Second, the ordering of poets and poems also affords the reader an historical overview of Israeli poetry since the 1940s.

Finally, an effort was made to include a sizable number of poems that had not yet been published in translation. It should be noted also that all the translations appearing here are the work of the coauthors of this volume; thus the anthology mirrors a purposeful artistic control. In each case, too, the poets themselves were consulted regarding the translations. Their direct involvement in the process of bringing these works before the reader has been a source of great pleasure and satisfaction.

Many debts of gratitude are due with respect to the compilation and completion of this book. First, our thanks to the poets, who gave considerably of their time and energies to review the various drafts of our translations and offered helpful suggestions and encouragement throughout the work process. We are grateful to the Hebrew Union College—Jewish Institute of Religion for making possible a number of visits to Israel, and to Spertus College of Judaica, Chicago, for several weeks' leave and a generous grant from the Dean's Fund, which allowed the authors to meet in Israel and to confer face to face with the poets. We are much obliged to our friend Dr. Uri D. Herscher, Executive Vice President of the College-Institute and Dean of its Los Angeles campus, for helping us meet the costs of securing permission to make use of copyrighted material. Thanks also are due to Mrs. Jacob Cohn and the Cohn Scholars Fund at Spertus College for a grant in support of this project. Deana Smith, Secretary to the Faculty and Dean at Spertus College, deserves plaudits for her unstinting assistance in typing the manuscript in its various stages, including the final draft. Our appreciation also goes to Reva Slaw of Spertus College, whose word-processing acumen was very helpful in the final retyping. The authors also wish to express their gratitude to all others—colleagues, students, and friends—who, over the years, read the translations and offered their helpful comments. Finally, our thanks and love to our wives and children, who gave of themselves, directly and indirectly, so that this work, itself a creative, gratifying labor of love, might be brought to fruition.

Notes to Introduction

1. Mark Twain, *The Innocents Abroad* (1869; reprint New York: Harper and Brothers, 1903), II, 329, 391–93.
2. Ibid., p. 264.

3. Shulamit Hareven, "Ha'im tihye sifrut bishnot ha'alpayim?" [Will there be literature in the third millennium?] *Yedi'ot Aḥaronot*, May 20, 1983.

4. Yoram Bronowski, "Romantikan zach me'od" [A very pure romanticist], *haArets*, July 22, 1983.

5. Natan Zach, *Kavei Avir* [Air lines] (Jerusalem: Keter, 1983), pp. 11ff.

6. Leslie A. Fiedler, *Waiting for the End* (New York: Stein and Day, 1964).

7. Ludwig Lewisohn, *Expression in America* (New York: Harper and Brothers, 1932), p. ix.

8. Gideon Katzenelson, *Le'an Hem Holkhim* [Where are they going?] (Tel Aviv: Alef, 1968). See also Simon Halkin, "Kirkhei shira tse'ira bashanim ha'aḥaronot" [Volumes of young poetry in recent years], *Beḥinot* I, 1 (1952): 8. Excerpts of the Halkin article also appeared in "Postscript: The Younger Poets," *Poetry* 92, 4 (July 1958): 259–65.

AMIR
GILBOA

 Amir Gilboa was born in 1917 in Radzivilov, a town
in the Ukrainian province of Volhynia. In his youth
Gilboa was taught Hebrew and the classical texts by
a local tutor in his home town. In his teen years he
spent time at a *hakhshara* encampment—a "pre-
paratory" village that readied Jewish youth for aliya
and life on a kibbutz. In late 1937, leaving his family behind, he joined a
group of forty who made a successful attempt at illegal immigration to
Mandatory Palestine. For several years he worked at a variety of jobs: in
orchards and quarries, on road-building projects, in Kibbutz Givat Hash-
losha, Netanya, and Petaḥ Tikva, and around British Army camps. Join-
ing the Eighth Army in 1942, he took part in the North Africa campaign
and the siege of Malta; later he saw action with the Jewish Brigade in
Italy. Demobilized in 1946, he was soon involved in Israel's 1948–49 War
of Independence. For twenty years Gilboa was a member of the editorial
staff of the Masada Publishing Company in Tel Aviv. In this role he was
able to encourage the publication of works by several of Israel's younger
poets. In 1982 he was awarded the Israel Prize for literature. Gilboa died
in Tel Aviv on September 2, 1984.

Reportedly, Gilboa returned from service in World War II with nearly
one hundred poems written on various battlefields. These works—in-
cluding the agonized elegies on the deaths of his parents, brothers, and
sisters, all victims of the Holocaust—formed the core of his first major

collection, *Seven Domains* (1949). It was the combined effect of this collection and his *Early Morning Songs* (1953) that established Gilboa as Israel's foremost younger poet. Thematically the poems of these two volumes embodied both a personal and a national transition from the chaos of Holocaust to the throes of statehood.

From the very beginning of his career Gilboa was identified with those writers who propounded a "new direction" for Israeli literature. In terms of poetic expression, this prospect signified a break with the Avraham Shlonsky—Natan Alterman style, a body of writing highly allusive, often euphuistic, replete with puns, and infused with the language of traditional Hebrew texts. Gilboa eventually moved away from these modes of expression; yet his earlier poems clearly demonstrate an indebtedness to the Shlonsky-Alterman heritage, especially in the emphatic use of an archaic, biblical diction. In Gilboa's works, however, Shlonsky's lush, evocative scenery becomes ironic, alluding more often than not to the harsh, unromantic plight of the pioneer settler. Poetry itself is a mixed calling, blending together the "flower" and the "fire," reflecting actual circumstances of loneliness, sacrifice, and despair.

The poetic tone in *Seven Domains* varies from the ecstatic to the elegiac to the lyrical. Ritualistic poems of investiture, sorrowful poems of familial mourning, poems of love and poems of vengeance—in these works of the forties Gilboa documents his personal progress as a poet, as a bereaved son and brother, as a confused, angry observer and rememberer of events beyond belief. In *Early Morning Songs* the language assumes a more colloquial, more proselike character, with less formal poetic structures and phrasing. The poetry is also more playful, with an abundance of close, internal rhymes, word plays, and even satirical comments. It is in this collection that Gilboa began writing his psychological portraits of biblical heroes—Moses, Joshua, Isaac, Saul—often endowing them with an anachronous awareness of future events, of tragic outcome. The poems in the last section of *Blues and Reds* (1963) show the poet's joyful embrace of nature. The rain, sun, and fields engender an intimate awareness of the common origin of all things, of the poetic imagination as well.

Most of the poems of *I Wanted to Write the Lips of Sleepers* (1968) are concerned with the act of writing poetry itself, with the poet's feelings about the power—or powerlessness—of expression. Taking the shape of pensées, the poems contemplate things beyond his control: life's swift passing, the impersonality of time, the dispensability of poetry, the poet's social and artistic isolation. At the center of these poems is the "dream," that ironic moment of insight which cannot be relived or adequately transmitted once the dreamer awakens. Of course, the poet himself is the dreamer, the one asleep. He is caught in a kind of thought-limbo between knowing and fear, insight and helplessness; he suffers conflict and ambivalence; he wavers between affirmation and negation. The poetic voice bespeaks an abiding ambiguity, which is marked especially by the poems' structure: many poems have no firm ending; verses are constituted of intermingled phrases that flow into one another without any clarifying punctuation. Reader and poet alike grope for coherence, for a proper sense of phrasing, a reasonable division of words.

Gilboa's last collection, *Gazelle I Send You* (1972), which includes several poetic responses to the Six-Day War of 1967, resembles in style the previous volume: unpunctuated verse, ambiguous phrasing, dualistic themes, a measured, pensive voice. But a difference is evident in the concrete objects employed to convey the poems' main topics. Nature again plays a central role in these poems, many of which express Gilboa's visions of time, memory, loneliness, and death. Flowers, birds, fields, the sea, stars, shrubs, the wind—Gilboa returns to these natural images, attempting through them to convey an enduring wonderment at the simple act of being alive. Consequently, the tone of these poems, though still fatalistic, is much more lyrical. The poet revels in the daily actions of others; he contemplates the essential unities of time, nature, and being; he recognizes both the folly and the painful necessity of remembering. What was evident throughout Gilboa's career characterizes the *Gazelle* collection, too: an astounding, sustaining vibrancy of poetic expression.

FROM *SEVEN DOMAINS* (1949)

A Death in Spring

Light flooding both banks
an excess of light.
Poured into ditches
into every pit.
Bringing forth more legends
but not letting them take place.
Mounting the stairs with us
to solve the riddle of this day.
All deaths reliant on it—
rushing back to its shelter.

Morning-Selah

All my friends will come shouldering salvation
Their spilled blood streaming toward their veins
From springs—
In their hearts resurrection storming
The valley brilliant
With the sanctity of shrouds
Unveiled to the secret of life.

All the mornings enfolded in darkness
For their sake, when daylight comes on,
Waving their swords in blessing
Laden with light and quiet—
For they've hidden their treasure till the moment appears
In the steps of kingdom.

Our Dreams

Proud and beaten we've passed the night.
Slivers of dreams fell on the sand
like hooves worn down, the horse has forgotten
where the smith had shod him—
But slivers of dreams will keep on coming
new and strange and powerful.
But slivers of dreams will overtake us, wounded,
devoid of light, at the cross of sunlight,
first to something as simple as breakfast.

We're so simple by day.
We're so sick by day.
But at night we scream at glories.
But at night our blood plots storms.
Our heads break through the walls and tile.
And by day we know we've dreamt secret things
and dream to recall the dream—
Messiah.

We're so big at night.
We scream a lot at night
from gardens of dread and madness.
We don't know all this,
we don't recall all this,
if not for the passers-by at night
terrified by our cries,
who tell us this
and run off in fear
a moment later.

FROM *EARLY MORNING SONGS* (1953)

I've Come to the Simplest Words

And what if someone comes and says: Here's the harp. Play for me on
    this harp.
Fool harp. Strings and rope. There's something higher than happiness.
    Something higher than grief.
Don't let me go. I'm so drunk from your wild words.
Wild words. Wild speech. Look at me I pray how straight are your
    words on my trestles.

I've come to the simplest words. Blessed be you, my trestles.

Kingdom of Silence

Cries still linger on the battlefield
and the High Priest gives thanks
for the victory. Piles of ashes
bear the news: the bloody summer is consumed.
Its firebrands fume now in words.
Silence settles. The throng's sounds
dim in the dusk.
Silence. The leaves are falling
falling. Soon it will be fall.

It will be so distant. All so distant.
The ground will all be
at peace again. The rain will fall again
on chimneys belching smoke. And suddenly
a storm will surge through the streams.

Winter. A fisherman readies his nets.
Spring will come. The waters will rise

and subside. From the banks the willow
will bow its branches. In the gardens
boughs will blossom. Young
eyes will rouse love
on the shore.
The view will take on a thousand shapes
in the eyes of a thousand in love.
The blazing summer will join them in
their resting place. Now it will lie torpid, and
now it will clamor with heat. It will call to battle.

Valiant echoes will answer the affliction
of voices. The butchers and the butchered.
Majestic mountains will pierce through
eyes from the dust. A fire
will flicker. Give off flame tongues. Flicker
tongues licking dust. A fire will
turn to ashes. Among smoking pages
parchment scrolls will sing praises
to a kingdom of silence. The sleeping will sing
praises to a kingdom of silence. Fragments
of lament sink
lower sink lower.
Stragglers will strike their tins.
The tins rattle. Fall
will cast down cast
down upon the fields. Upon the roads. All things
bound in books will be at rest. Selah. All the
generations will be at rest. Selah. Opaque-
eyed firebrands
are silent
silent are
the legions.

And there's no one else to come. No one
else to flee. No voice
for the dead to bequeath their will.
And one alone is left, standing still.

FROM *BLUES AND REDS* (1963)

I Love This Sunlight Cold

I love this sunlight cold in spaces transparent turning blue
As if all within me were calm and turning sacred for celestial
   celebration.
No words. Not out of expectance of hidden being.
This is being in itself. Slight in its breadth. Fragrant odorless in its
   pungency
And only one problem to wrestle somehow to walk on so
It will never change.
But all that time one primal knowledge—
Like before a creation after which nothing needs creating.
Like some presence ahover with timeless echoes of soul palaces
They're mountains of mountains of air of before becoming
And forever.

Rain Falls and Floods

Rain falls and floods, says the heart
And distantly distantly there drips in it
An ancient lament, moss so
Green at its edges,
And ancient sound of gold
That deceived it
That was lost and remained
That valley that mountain
That sun that
It held in it
That returned to it
When rain fell and flooded
And distantly in it
A pipe sang.

Ancient Song

My being not yet done
Already primeval and distant
From poems I dreamt while young
Poems wild and rampant

For a thousand years are a sudden quake
As against an eternal day—
When those rising up and digging down
With a single stroke
Sky and abyss would sing.

The Ends of Things

The ends of things were heard no more
Once they fell to earth
And turned to dust.
And the gloom of firmament rained and rained.

All things turned gray cleansed
Dwarfed inside a horizon closing off, closing off.
Only the burning bush flared guarding
Our clenched fists.

But it went up in flame
Against the brightening day.

And we've nothing more to say.

Watchful Wakeful

The rain would fall on me
And split the earth
I'd stretch my leg roots
Into the deep
And grasp as with pliers
The world's foundations.

The rain would fall and fall
From every place my roots
Would call out
Abyss to abyss

Waters gathering
Wedding sea
Poem ever-dwelling
Depths
Quietly
A poem buds
Waters darkness
Echoes

Oh, this joy uncontained
Silence
To bear
The weight of the thrill
Watchful
Wakeful
For the rain that
Would fall on me.

FROM *I WANTED TO WRITE THE LIPS OF SLEEPERS* (1968)

I'll grab hold of a butt of dream.
I mustn't let it touch my lips.
Mustn't even remember so much
For I might still fall ill.
Alas, daughter of Jerusalem.

I've forgotten whose glory would not fail
In the tangle of shrubs asleep.
I've always known this. Like a telltale scar.
Until one day I revived as if after seventy years.

And no more may one gently move the sleepers' lips.
The years fill each doorstep with malediction.
On the table a glass of smoking dreams
Just a bit longer my poor eyes I'll not
See it.

⋘⋙

Of late from time to time there's risen
Within me a chorus marking time in fast tempo
Even before the anesthetist begins
Counting I'm asleep but to my sorrow
There's no more surgery to do for again there's
Nothing that's why I know I'll
Not come again. I'll not come. I know already.

And you too though
Unknowing

≈§≈

Until recently there was fear
Now fear's an old acquaintance
Through its boldness now the distant
Myths again are whispered in my ear. In its antique look too
It's stranger than lost remembrance and on no account
Delights in causing fright. A great savant quickly
Discovered my unripened fruits and made them his hosts

And highhandedly insists on sharing my bed.

≈§≈

I pray from the heart a prayerbook
Its margins torn and all the missing words I
See them flying off they've been flying off a long while
Seeking a footrest how
Shall I bring them healing and the heart
Of my prayerbook its margins eaten away
Spent and naked

≈§≈

I press pen to paper like a pistol to the temple
Now with a single squeeze I'll shoot to the last all the days and nights.
No. I won't shoot until this moment, maybe this moment alone
And those that follow will quickly go on running without me.

Whose solace is space that is eternity.

ᴥᵇᶾᶾᵇᴥ

This isn't what I want to write I
write the words dry as after
the wind's dried up all the rain-
filled puddles once I'd have said blue now
it's a nameless unremembered hue
long ago I forgot the names of all
colors and it's better that colors belong to children
and better that I tell children to care for them better
than I or at least leave them beyond the high
mountain, where is that mountain, which, if they pass it no more
no one will pass over to them for
why should a stranger pass through the gates of rivers
singing at the entries of Edens in the clefts
of rocks better that they become mountain goats ever
free and surefooted never stumbling as they leap
over the lips of the abyss

And what if they're no more the mountain goats

ᴥᵇᶾᶾᵇᴥ

I wanted to write the lips of sleepers
And I saw they're really all asleep
And there won't be anyone to hear my heart's awake
And I was terrified
And my hands went limp

ᴥᵇᶾᶾᵇᴥ

That very day I saw that is we saw
the end of all wars blurring more becoming
more obscure and lost forever with them. So be it. Amen.
That very night I saw that is we saw

the joyful fire on every mountaintop scatter
the darkness which to this very instant had alarmed
the legends still left after their listeners
were murdered. The legends. Where are they.

❧❦❧

Yes, I caught the butterfly. Went crazy for the moment.
What is this, back and forth, it got away
Dodged my hand.
I saw the butterfly. Maybe the butterfly saw me.
But something, maybe someone, neither of us saw.
I call the butterfly butterfly. Don't know
What the butterfly might call me.
But something, maybe someone, neither of us would comprise.
The butterfly was tricky, but I, this time, was quicker.
What shall we call the one immeasurably quicker than either of us.
It flitted the butterfly flitted from flower to flower.
In mid-course, this time, my hand sprang out and caught it.
How slow we were both of us as against the one quicker than either.
I saw the butterfly. Maybe the butterfly saw me.
Whose eye caught both of us before this.
I sense him watching us
From every side at once
In a rush ever flaming, forming.

I don't know what name to call him.

❧❦❧

In a night hour this is how the things are written. And now night.
   And now alone.
Look, as soon as morning comes light will flow over you too.
It's good that no one sees you now. That no one sees you alone.
That now it's night. And keep your breathing steady.
Tomorrow, as soon as morning comes, light will flow over everything.
   Over you too.

But hold on tonight. All night.
If you're not afraid of wanderings, wherever they may lead, which
    suddenly
you'll remember even if you've never seen them before, but
they've been destined for you for a long while, with memory's creation,
if you're not afraid of all these, lie down and sleep.
And you might want to go out to meet them. To greet them.
You won't wrestle with them. You'll be carried off, rather you'll be swept
up with them. What will your face look like on your return.
If you're not afraid, lie down and sleep.
You'll rise one with them all. At last all will go well with you too.
A tiny grain in the dunes. As it lies so will it lie. As it blows so will it
    blow.
Praise man.

FROM *BALM* (1971)

With the Rain

I'll still walk with the rain open and dreaming
To a journey that passed and forgot me on the road
Knowing for certain that with this hand I've untied
The knot and set my horses loose to graze in the meadow
Before my memory flowers will wither
There in the patches of earth digging and digging
My many wells the fear of an end
That's opened and opened with a wail unending
While open and dreaming I'll still walk with the rain.

Havdala

At this hour of nightfall
Again I dream of solace.
For I've promised myself so little.
For I've not done for myself so much.

God forbid that I find it in the promise
That God made to Abraham
That God made to Isaac
That their seed shall multiply as the sand
On the seashore
So many.

For I'm not Abraham
For I'm not Isaac
For I've promised myself so little.
For I've not done for myself so much.

For I am unsound
For I am but sand
So little of so much.

My Soul Wanders About

My soul wanders about
In the streets of an errant city
Of life's summing up.
Who said put away
Thy finery and thy silken robes
For thou art come to thine end
And to dust thou shalt return
For from dust camest thou
Naked and naked art
Thou and thy mother too, and surely
My soul from naught hath woven
The chain of her stars
And with stuff of heaven and of hell
Is the metal of her bones taken shape.
Her flesh is her own
Her being her bone.

Come quiet here
A new creating
Posing puzzles to the questioned.

Will one arise to command
Her end.

FROM *GAZELLE I SEND YOU* (1972)

gazelle I send you to the wolves not in the wood they're
in the city too on sidewalks run from them the panic
in your lovely eyes they envy me watching how
you leap up in fright and your breath

I send you into the thick of the battle
the war's no more for me

my heart gazelle at the look of you wandering bloodstained in the dawn

My left hand's like after a vow. It hurts. I'm trying to dream again.
If it's where it should be. Will it obey. If it does I'll command it again.
Where are the hand phylacteries to be my reins of long life.
And straps to bind my arm with. To be outstretched for me again.
To bring a dream again against this heart rebelling to slow down at
    dawn.

Grown pale cold, the hair on my arm stiffens. And I mislead myself
I swear I'll try to count each and every hair, one by one
as if my fated life's suspended before me until at last
I'm lost, laughing at life's reckoning, life that should it rise for me
    between
night and day I'll call it my own once more. If I'm where I should be.

This whole land belongs to me sleeping and awake I see
one long electric flash of a dream making

flocks of swallows flutter on the tree boughs
weaving the window and my flesh and bones onto
a dizzy wind over an immense land
which all belongs to me.

❧

They'll all get up. I know I see them
getting up turning homeward each one
eyeing the way he remembers
and his tiny hesitation undoes the distance
and links distances together magically like a dream
whether dreamt or not. And even so
the woman's already laughing through her tears
and his children are rubbing cheeks with him
and telling him their tale
which he expected to hear once more
after it was whispered in his ear
by the mouths of gaping roots

❧

My city mine. No more can I
enter your gates my city
without my city mine with me in you.
Worn, ashamed, I'll lower my eyes
if I take a step in you,
be it but one my city and not toward my city
to know that with me in you
you'd be my city mine.
For you'll be taken from me my city
without my city mine with me in you, my city
if it were taken from me.

❧

To come free to a city under siege
safe to wander its streets
to come free to a city under siege
safe to leave the city
and to see and to know there's no
city that's

❧

I looked outside. Pools of water.
Strands of silt between each pool
Sprouting with stems of hands
unvoiced
fish were cast ashore
their eyes behind them
in the water watching me still
terrified I run off run and run
beneath me and above I'm caught in
my throat my voice
is hidden between the waters

❧

When I'm by myself I don't know. But I
expect no answer.
But I can't sum it up. Maybe so I won't panic.
But, to tell the truth, that's not why.
That's why it hasn't occurred to me.
But that's why it's my fate to be cast forth
over many waters. A tycoon.
His riches are without measure.
His ways without limit.
So that no one will know the way I left,
if I left,

and whoever comes looking for me won't know
whether to look among the dead
or among the living.

❧

Back and forth. As in a swing. When there's
neither strength nor interest to go on swinging.
But still, one could fall. To the ground.
But from this immense lassitude,
this lack of interest,
still, like a limb somehow kept alive,
there's a sense sharp as a sea of boiling lime
ready to burn and be burned. To consume and
be consumed. And, in fact, this is what a
butterfly gains for its brief day, it sucks
and is sucked into the very end.

❧

I guess it will come suddenly. And every
acid trick of fate will demand a certain pragmatic
meaning. Of midday terrors. Better, if only
to come out all right, even brilliantly,
if only there'd be someone like you, someone who remembers.
When it's all over. Even when it's all over,
there'll be someone lying in wait at every stop
telling your story along with
the wind. Your story retold later will be all right.
Your story retold later will be all right, just as you always wanted.
When each stop was only a sign, a phony name,
which now, even now, will still exist, will be covered
when everything's perfectly visible but there's
nothing more to see,
one man, what will he remember

⋅⊱⊰⋅

To run a night's distance, distances by night, nothing's easier than
    traveling distances
by night nothing's easier, for no obstacle appears before you at night,
for whatever's before you is behind you a dense meadow
no ups no downs at night a knife cuts
the murk a ball slices the blind tree a mole
at the heart of black being burrows to tear
a screen whose thickness despite everything
extends to the edge of daylight
and won't be revealed to the eyes of one
whose world has gone dark.

⋅⊱⊰⋅

a city defenseless by day one sees desolation
makes distances clear to you
by night from every side
legions rise up rise up against you
a city defenseless by day your name
expands endlessly
at night it shrinks it shrinks
and your name is minute in your midst

⋅⊱⊰⋅

Times stir in me uncalendrically, chaotically,
someone in me dresses and undresses, is,
without my being asked, the answer always in his mouth
these clothes of yours these clothes of yours
all yours they are
you were born unceasingly are born

Even on a morning like this yours is gray

ABBA
KOVNER

Much of Abba Kovner's poetry consists of extended dramatic poems or cycles of poems that combine a poignant lyricism with symbolic imagery. Mainly a symbolist poet, Kovner demonstrates an affinity both with the masters of Russian modernism (Blok, Yesenin) and especially with Natan Alterman (1910–70), whose uses of dramatic dialogue, mythic figures, and biblical diction have permeated Kovner's works.

Kovner was born at Sevastopol, in the Crimea, in 1918. His family had been stopped on their way to Israel by the outbreak of World War I. Soon afterwards, they returned to Vilna, the Lithuanian capital, where Kovner was raised in the tradition of left-wing Zionism. During the Nazi occupation, he became a leader of the partisan groups fighting the Germans, and later, after the war, he helped organize the flow of Jewish survivors to Israel. He wrote his first collection of poetry in 1947 while imprisoned by the British (for illegal immigration) in Egypt and Jerusalem. Since 1947 he has been a member of Kibbutz Ein Haḥoresh. Kovner has published a number of prose works along with his several books of poetry, and in 1970 he was awarded the Israel Prize for literature. During the seventies he was a prime force in organizing the Diaspora House (Beit Hatefutsot), a museum of Jewish history at Tel-Aviv University.

The predominant backgrounds of Kovner's works are the desert, the battlefield, natural landscapes, primitive rites, Ein Haḥoresh, and Jerusa-

lem. The pervasive setting, however, is a visionary one. By projecting
memory and experience—of the Holocaust, Israel's wars, his family, and
the land—through dreamlike scenes, Kovner creates in his poetry an
emotive immediacy and a mythic grandeur. The central images and voices
convey a shared experience of personal and national dimensions. The
little sister, the beloved, the mother and son, the burnt city, the heroic but
fearful fighter—these figures and the relationships among them inject the
poems with passions that express forcefully the vulnerability of Jewish
existence. The poetic voice constantly is called upon to bear witness to
the innocents' pathetic struggle to survive.

Evoking the lofty and intimate tone of the Songs of Songs, the poems of
Canopy in the Desert (1970) constitute a homily on the fate of the Jewish
people in recent history. The narrator-wanderer-bridegroom seeks to wed
his beloved sister-city-bride in the desert. Through these mythic personae
Kovner unites the Holocaust with the 1967 Six-Day War in a symbolic
vision of threatened existence and confirmed life. Destruction and conti-
nuity are perceived as an unending rite, and Kovner's use of liturgical
structures and biblical allusions continually stresses this ritualistic sense
of history.

Even in the more lyrical and pensive *Of All My Loves* (1965), the
imagery tends to be symbolic. The blend of intimate love poems, nature
lyrics, and dream-visions of the Holocaust only strengthens the impres-
sion that love and beauty are but temporary respites from memory. The
world in general lacks a needed humanism. The realms of science and
God seem cold and remote; the faults are moral and cosmic, not just
historic. Here and in his later collections, *Observations* (1977) and *To*
(1980), Kovner shares with his readers poignant reminiscences, percep-
tions of society and its values, and a lyrical awareness of the inexorable
processes in history and life. He asserts both the despair inherent in his
poetic endeavor and the hopefulness that the endeavor generates by
warding off the sadness, by "delaying the tearing asunder" of his mourn-
ful soul.

FROM *OF ALL MY LOVES* (1965)

Of All My Loves

A sky unshaken, smokeless   ashless
will turn blue again, a headrest of memory for me
                                    O my soul, be thankful
that of all my loves
    I've saved from trampling this one flower fallen
between the album pages

Accuse me not aloud!
Of all I own,
I left for safeguard
in the customshouse
only two teeth of a comb
    a greasy hat
a tongueless shoe like a mouth unquestioning
    and a bundle
of names like a camel's freight;

    they didn't die for me   I didn't
    die beneath their weight;   one day when your womb
        gave me up to love
    the lovers came in smoke   O you their creator,
    it's a waste to weep   for me. I'm not the only
    one to lose the world. What do we know anyway?
Look, the flower dead between the album pages
    returns root-
less to life:

The Scientists Are Mistaken

The scientists are mistaken, the universe
was not created eons ago.
The universe, I maintain, is created every day.

The scientists are mistaken when they claim
the universe was shaped from one primeval clay,
I maintain the universe is shaped every day
from diverse materials with nothing in common;
only the ratio of their masses, like
that of the element sorrow and the element hope,
makes them companions
and curbstones. I much regret

the need to stand up in all humility, to challenge
what is so well accepted by the experts,
that the greatest of velocities is that of light.
But I and my radiated flesh
quite recently experienced something else
whose speed exceeds even the speed of light
and returns surely, not in a straight line,
because of the convolutedness of creation
or the perfection of the Name

And if we combine all this into a proper equation,
perhaps
it will explain why I refuse to believe that your voice
and everything I set before myself eternally
and everything that was so real and suddenly
was lost
was really lost forever.

And if the world has not yet been constructed from it,
every day there is blessing.

How Many Poems Were Lost

How many poems were forever lost
when I closed my eyes to kiss your lips:

Whose heads were knocked against the wall for fear
of nights white at the doorways to your rooms:

Which danced over the unhearing waves to the abyss
when in vain they sought a signal from your ports:

Which went forth as doves and returned as ravens
burnt from approaching your borders:

Like knives they rose. Like ships they burned and the
(cursed cursed) sound left your eyes shut:

If a poem proceeds in blood—from me and within me
your thousand murderers have risen up:

Your neck I throttled then   with a poem:
Your huge face I seized   with a poem:
Your two breasts I
squeezed like grape clusters   into a poem:
Nor mankind shall I spare I said   a poem:

They're lost. All of them. The earth
is cleft. I've reached your lips:

Lord of Dreams

We're not silent!
You alone are silent.
Give proper repose
to the outcry and the hope. For look,
we've not many choices
save this one chance
to reach out,
when all is said
and done,
to the beautiful, to fill
with the blood a sacred cup
wherewith the spirit is refreshed
and fortified to go
back
directly
    to the world

The Voice of My White City

To Y. B-M.*

If only you'd seen if only you'd seen
how in windblown sand
there came down to the sea
the silence you wept

and he saw. And imagined he'd seen
you in your fullness, from nearby,
and like this flower he sought only
to raise up your shadow
and you, a stone of the street.

* Yocheved Bat-Miryam, Hebrew poet, 1901–80.—TRANS.

FROM *CANOPY IN THE DESERT* (1970)

The Hour's Late

Bare earth it is, the way to my love.
I come to her as to a rendezvous.
In silence I try to build on its ruins
a transparent city. To float houses astray
in two-lane streets. To restore their façades,
making them as orderly as crop rotation,
letting the sea burst inside into the tiny
square rooms to rinse the windows alternately
of frost buds and strips of sand,
as would a long relied on housemaid. Already—

there's a highway.
A traffic light.
I can go now. Just let me hang
my hat on the swaying bough of an acacia, let me
fit my eyes with new traffic lights so they won't shut
at bad times. I've already tied my tie
to the neck of the wooden cock,
the tie with a pure gold pin
left me by my father. I'm still spreading out
my coat before the first policeman's dog
arrives on time running before his master. But my shoes
please let me leave my shoes
for the cat
until a better fairytale's found
for the children of the city
and you
you alone, little sister, I'll take with me
on my back. Carrying you across
my strip of bare earth.

FROM *THE RHYTHM BAND APPEARS ON MOUNT GERIZIM* (1972)

11

Between mountains coils a city. Wind
encircles the face of the blessèd. Wind heaps up a mound
to placate the Mountain of Curse.
O city
before whom do you stand now
face to face
for your fate. A shutter: A shutter: Peer
through the crack and see, he's coming back.
He who's offered no reward for fears
an infant
wide-eyed steps
from the shadowed forest path

and measures. Wherever he
measures
the distance between him and his shadow
shrinks.

His midday. And his fingers tremble
from the dread of safety and distrust.
Will a surfeit of love make him murder you tomorrow.

(Drums)
(Drums)

City! Up with you up
speak a poem through him:

FROM *THE LITTLE BOOK* (1972)

Sun-Watchers

Eat and drink
Eat   and drink because
tomorrow we're not going to die   because
we're going to live   because
we're going to go through the whole twilit city
from end to end
that Hebrew city between the veiled hills because
you stand revealed
with me by your side,
my beautiful bridegroom:
we sun-watchers lie down in the   field
we'll be. And until the sun shines
on the wall again we'll lie down again mouth   to mouth
and anyone who's seen it all and said nothing
will see   again
under the tree's spreading boughs
how love is torn
you and I and the canopies overhead
are seven,
my beautiful bridegroom.

Dinosaurs

Dinosaurs wept angry tears
crocodiles weep floods:
a Jew who loves a woman
mourns her passing with Kaddish.

He says Kaddish but only his lips move,
the decree moves on mutely before him.

A white swan sings within his heart's walls,
silence sheathes his frame.

When moist silence enfolds the earth
and wreathes his neck with ribbons,
then for seven days a Jew sings this song,
his voice tapping on a tiny door:

Forty years of silence we kept between us,
dear love, now we'll talk together in tears.
And may He who makes peace on high be kind to him,
may He lift him from his grief, may He make him glad.

FROM *OBSERVATIONS* (1977)

Dimmed Observation

The night's still silken. Curtains spread red silk
In slow motion from the edge of dream. Both of us awake
Try quietly to splice the thread
Snuffed out between the ribs. It scares me
To watch this rain
Beat against the windows.

And still the night
Within is silken. Your breath a silent glade
Guarding its frontier. When unbelieving I
Count the number of beats
And notate them my eye all
At once discovers my body (are your arms outstretched?) naked
Laid out
Inside and outside
The sheets (somehow they must be gathered up!)
Something twitches in my chest and doesn't wane
When the winter rain climbs on the windows.

Rain—
It's only rain! Like an oath I repeat
For the third time, it's not your blood.
It's then my finger runs over your neck
Poking about like a stick held out before a blind man.

Lookout on a Rock on the Heights of Mount Hermon

1.

This is the naked rock. Right here. From here
we had a fine view of the city and the land and

the treeless waterless boulders.
Here he knelt and watched
his fear crumbling opposite the terror. A cliff split
like fingers spread to bless
the wayfarer. No, there's no sign
of a grave here. Only wonder
only puzzlement.

2.

You lived the things which came later and I
sat here paralyzed my eyes scratching
the stones scattered below
scattered shapes and signs of those
who'd been my friends and enemies a while ago.
So I gathered their remains from the plain
to sort them in the sun—
We stopped here. At exactly 4:25 A.M.
someone woke us to say it
was time to move toward
the voices you'd see even in the blindness
of your death. For wander where it will
the eye that follows them
will never break away.

3.

And at night. Only at night suddenly in your arms
it's like it was then when we left the southern front: you'll
live these things as they happen and I mindless quiet
with a filthy fingernail still scratch on your belly
shapes and signs now ended
scattered and torn each one
will confront his fate

In the lookout.

I Don't Know if Mount Zion

1.

I don't know if Mount Zion would recognize itself
in the fluorescent light at midnight
when all that remains of Jerusalem
is her beauty wakeful
in the milky light spreading over her limbs
still wings raising it above the desert which sank away
so slowly above the stars
this eerie seashell floating from the midst of night
a transparent giant
so much sky sweeping over it
I don't know if Mount Zion looks
into my heart which holds its breath now behind a latticed window
out of torment and delight and for whom it's meant
in the heart of night

2.

These olive trees
which never bowed with the hidden knowledge
and the grooved wrinkles this whole blue fan
over the Gehenna road
I don't know if Mount Zion sees the things
that changed our image
beyond recognition. The hands that touched it daily
like a mother touching her son's forehead fell
elusively into the slumber
of the Dead Sea
Does it hear the cry
from the Marketplace of Gates or the thrust of my prayer from the
    shade—
What good are friends who watch from the balcony
while our heart wrestles on the stage
and what use are we poets if we
don't know how to speak
—Does Mount Zion really exist or
is its light like our love beaming from a source
rising every
night

Vow

When I put on my hat. When I get into my shoes again.
When the city comes near and her night is plague.
When the breath of your mouth melts from my lips
And Earth resumes spinning on its axis.
And you're able no longer to make out my face
And we won't know each other—always
Like a sudden bough of lilac
The smell of your body
Will linger
(The Mountain of Three Crosses and the Veila* my ensigns)
For I'll wear it an eternal flowering from here
To my final springtime.

*The district in which the Arch of Titus is located in Rome.—TRANS.

Front Page

A 1976 Ford. A shiny lacquered
Mercedes. "Viking" seeks a foothold
On Mars. The Russian astronauts have shaved.
For sure. To live
In the sea, to be
In silence, Cousteau said from the "Calypso"
Lebanon they're still in the news
Those left
For later. The Sixth Fleet moves toward
The Cape of Good Hope. An encore for Julie Andrews.
In the new Palace—("My Fair Lady." Exalted among widows,
The world's not ungrateful! They gave him a great funeral
The entire nation escorted the cortege of the slain
Conductor) "The Lover" in the small hall, before its closing
On account of the Value Added Tax. At the Cameri:
"A Man For All Seasons."
I'm not a man for all seasons. I'm trying without prejudice
To comprehend this season
Before the appearance of the next
Fire.

On My Words

On every defeat on every design they've walked with necks outstretched
   meticulously

Making their way with tiny, measured steps up and down
Scattering vows on every miraculous hill
Too clever to understand it's possible
To be complete in you
The right to be
Deceived
And betrayed

By this. And to rise. As one coming to flowers. To plant anew. You. In
   joy bursting
With lust. For oblivion. For remembrance. Let them live. Beautiful in
   their blood they'll live
For shock. And to stand hand on mouth
Agape.

And to know that after this after all this
The fear
Of return:

FROM *TO* (1980)

To the Things That Are Immortal

Suddenly there stirs in you the image of parks in polaroid colors like
Take a photo:
A smooth-planed wooden bench in the shade of fanning oaks.
Nasturtium hungrily seizes
The remnant of sun moving over the green bridge:
Time to turn back.
And a flat-heeled shoe (you loved it so) in the soft sand
Still scribbles a stubborn picture
Puzzle. A barefaced knee didn't hesitate
To say what the two held back,
The same old story: he 19 she 17 on the wooden bench
In the Bernardine garden. A hand's
First touch
And the sound of water forced against the dam
Painlessly about to burst.

From a field ploughed in sweat rise memories of things
That are immortal: a carnation stem crushed
In your lips. A lock of hair
Fallen over your eye
And fake pearl buttons which
Fastened a blue-checked dress, in a close row
Like an imaginary breakwater.
And her earlobe still pierced (there's a tiny shop
In Glaziers Street where you can buy pretty earrings
On credit)—a foolish smile. A flat-heeled shoe
A knee whispering, white. You know
You knew her.
But you're no longer able to recall this face.
You know you mustn't take in vain the bitterness
And the name. But it's foolish to pretend
There's something like conscience
In a world which erased this face with Zyklon B.

Poem: Alte Zachen

1

Father wore an overcoat with a narrow velvet collar.

2

Underneath as needed a striped suit and always a well
ironed shirt.

3

Sadness lay on his clothing even then like a permanent
crease.

4

There was no radio in the house. But his curiosity knew no
bounds
His mind awake at night roved
everywhere.

5

In his time he'd correctly calculated the outcome
of the Russo-Japanese War, a trifle late.

6

He loved potato kugel with herring

7

When no herring was to be had he made do
with beets.

8

Suddenly it was over, the First World War
A year later it was Year One
for Polish independence, suddenly in 1919
he inherited a stone house

9

In the capital. On the riverbank, with 22
ramshackle flats. But though he was a
bigshot, with his tenants

10

And his creditors

11

His love was still
the potato kugel his wife
made for every occasion:

12

They loved the sea
whose waters had begun to reflect
another country

13

He dreamed of going back

14

. . . .

15

When he went back. On the very day he imagined
his father's return
he lost his voice. And more.

16

He was standing on the threshold.

17

And he had no witness to see
Father life-size
how he still stood on the threshold

18

Oblivious to time. How long
his mouth remained wide open

19

And silent.
Until he moved his lips. Until his tongue regained
its use, until it was once more his voice
and echo:
             Father

20

Behind a muslin drape and the boy
buzzing in his head.

21

From that day on he felt his head
buzzing. Like fragments of heart rubbing his temples
and not always only

22

       When an uninvited guest came by.
There and not there. Or
when playing with his grandson: a splendid soap bubble
with all the rainbow colors about to burst on the
windowscreen
          Or then
at once this buzzing in his head!

23

Luckily, the pain vanishes just as it comes.
So often
nothing takes its place.

Tashlich

On the first of Tishre I was walking the field in the evening breeze.
Suddenly I found myself looking around
Searching for a well.

My father was no more. He would turn his pockets inside out and say
"And all their sins you shall cast into the deep"—
It's a field of Ein Haḥoresh. And I'm alone in the field
No veteran, no oldtimer. My pockets filled with
Sand and gravel, and why "all their sins"
Why won't it suffice
    "Into the deep"
        For him who knows how to ask
For him who was
Incinerated
He had the boldness to ask how shall we save ourselves
And how does Satan unrepentant save
Himself
    And the Creator
        Who created him in his image?

I'd walk in the field in the evening breeze in relative serenity
If it weren't the first of Tishre
And in the field I'm so
Alone.

UNCOLLECTED

While at Prayer

In his grief
And the wind still
In his hair
While on the keys
Of a Hermes-3000 without foe
Without struggle his fingers
Would fall
Among letters recoiling like
The heart, letters slowly turning dark

Until there'd come
And rise up like the dew
A final sweeping
Line
Torn like his ravaged world

Then comforted he'd get up
And go forth to meet
His oncoming
Day

To his garden
Open
To the elliptic hills
In the gladelike landscape
Made of imported soil watered
With tears and laughter, with strength
And a harmonica
Then in his window
A rainbow in the cloud:

Sprinklers prattled all that night
The violet expanse
In Elul and the banal cares
Of the island

—Where does he live?
                    In the forgotten storm
Did his transparent lovers there learn
Only to fall as one
Or in the fire's glow
Here
Opposite
The malignant flame?

Uncomprehending!
To be with
Them all. And alone
In the quiet of the house. Like a curtain
Kissing the distance
Saying in the rush of prayer:
God protect! The tears
And the laughter

                    And blood
A last line opens
To the depth
A line from which and in which his memory
Will never

Be lost—

HAIM GOURI

 As did most young Hebrew poets in the 1940s, Gouri cast his early works in the stylistic mold of Shlonsky, Alterman, and Lea Goldberg (1911–70). The poetry exhibited regular rhythm and rhyme, an archaic diction for lofty effect, a tendency toward plaintive nature lyrics, and a recurring female image representing an intimate other: the beloved companion, the sympathetic listener, the innocent victim, and, often, the land and its people. Adding to these elements a collective voice and a heroic tone, Gouri created moving hymns, elegies, and ballads that expressed the fears, the courage, and the bereavement born of the situations he faced during World War II and Israel's War of Independence.

Beyond the influence of the modern Hebrew masters, Gouri's work demonstrates an affinity with contemporary French literature, which he studied in the early fifties at the Hebrew University and at the Sorbonne. Aside from his literary achievement, Gouri's career has been in journalism, with long-time columns in the newspapers *Lamerḥav* and *Davar* and continuous, artful reportage of nationally significant events.

Haim Gouri was born in Tel Aviv in 1923. As a teenager he was educated at Kaduri, the renowned Israeli agricultural school. A member of the Palmach (the elite commando corps of the "Haganah," forerunner of the Israel Defense Forces) from 1942 to 1947, he rose in rank during the War of Independence and, since then, has served as an officer in the Israeli

Reserves. At the end of the world war he participated in the European missions of the Haganah and helped organize the flow of Jewish survivors into DP camps and to Palestine. This experience has never been erased from his mind. In nearly every book he has written, Gouri returns to Holocaust scenes and impressions. His first novel, *The Chocolate Deal* (1965), is a Beckett-like allegory of pathos and absurdity in postwar Berlin; in 1962, he wrote a journalistic account of the Eichmann trial; and in the 1970s he became a prime mover in producing the Holocaust film *The 81st Blow*. He also helped produce *The Last Sea*, a documentary film on the illegal immigration of Jews to Israel during the Mandate period.

Since *Flowers of Fire* (1949), Gouri has published more than half a dozen collections of verse. His poetry is in the main romantic and lyrical, displaying in its central voices a pensive, somber awareness of the world's inner workings. Serene landscapes give rise to poignant memories and emotions. Sadness, tears, quietude, night, dawn, flowers, lovers, and death are recurrent motifs that indicate Gouri's aesthetic romanticism. In *Compass Rose* (1960), he began developing a more personal emblem: the historical poem. Borrowing personalities and locales of the ancient world (Odysseus, Ithaca, Samson, Jerusalem), he blends antique and contemporary scenes to highlight a lingering sense of the heroic, a condition inevitably undermined by reality and time.

The ancient hero theme—often offset by Gouri's mocking jargon from the realms of business and journalism—is expanded in the *Movement to Touch* poems (1968). In this collection the dominant poetic images are the city, the kingdom, the prophet, and the poet. In the Bible, prophets and kings are often at odds; in Gouri's metaphorical scheme, the patterns are similarly counterpoised. The prophet usually symbolizes the contemplative witness, whose visions come to an ambiguous end: they bespeak great insight but proclaim a frustrating powerlessness. Thus, prophecy and poetry are parallel efforts. Like the prophet, the poet is acutely aware that most unhappy situations are beyond his (or any individual's) control. Both speak their words in the wind; both become self-doubting, vulnerable seers whose more lucid comprehension leads less to elation than to despair.

The later *Geḥazi* poems (1974; Geḥazi was the servant of the prophet Elisha)—untitled and more flowing, thus more visionlike—continue to explore this impotent intuitiveness. The culprit is the "kingdom," the oppressive political and historical forces that overwhelm the "city" and the "bride"—Gouri's symbols for security, place, and value. These figures cannot withstand the onslaughts of war and pain; they mourn humanity's essential transience. Relating in these poems mainly to the Six-Day War and its aftermath, Gouri again utilizes the female image; it both absorbs and reflects the poet's anguished disquietude, a mood that prevails despite his refined view of reality and of self. The same image recurs in the collection *Terrible* (1979), with the woman providing an anchor for reminiscences of missions and battles long over, for lyrical impressions of places and nature, and, above all, for an almost visionary attitude of historical destiny. Repeated allusions to biblical passages combine with fragments of memory that affirm the revealed power "of the hand which / long ago / shaped the passion and the pain."

FROM *COMPASS ROSE* (1960)

Mistake

The fly is brushed off the pale forehead
There are no candles to light at dusk.

Hour passes on to hour
Voices mimicking voices heard the day before.

The fly is brushed off the pale forehead
The feather quivers with the test.

The iron won't lapse into rusty silence
There's still room for imaginings.

What comes later can't be rushed
The diggers aren't sent out for nothing.

A gesture beckoning the unforeseen
A gesture beckoning the uncertain smiles.

◈

It seems to me I'm watching over walls
Of a city long dead.

Lights shining on me now
Are legacies of a light gone out long ago.

I walk among the things that time has left,
A passerby.
And they live without time slowly crumbling in the clocks.

They come back to me, back to live more slowly.
Alongside ashtrays,
Alongside cups of coffee grown cold.

I walk a lot and speculate
And benefit from the doubt

But I'm watching over walls of a city long dead.

His Mother

It was years ago, at the end of Deborah's Song,
I heard the silence of Sisera's chariot so long in coming,

I watch Sisera's mother peer out the window,
A woman with a silver streak in her hair.

This is what the maidens saw: A spoil of multi-hued embroidery,
Multi-hued embroideries two for the throat of each despoiler.
That very hour he lay in the tent as one asleep
His hands quite empty.
On his chin traces of milk, butter, blood.

The silence was not broken by horses and chariots.
Even the maidens fell silent one after another.
My silence reached out to theirs.
After a while sunset.
After a while the afterglow is gone.

Forty years the land knew peace. Forty years
No horses galloped, no dead horsemen stared glassily.
But her death came soon after her son's.

Piyyut for the New Year

To [the poet] Aharon Meirovitz

No this isn't a road intersected by enemy lines or foreign tongues or
    silence.
Neither I nor my voice is bound to observe these distances.
I walk and am not slain.
I come at last to a house. Stop. Knock at the door.

Every forgiving man says, What was, was. I keep coming back.
Every forgiving woman stands on a balcony sooner or later and waits
    for his return.
There's a window which isn't black. A letter which isn't lost enroute.
And if it didn't arrive yesterday it's sure to arrive tomorrow.

Every city is open tonight. Not under siege, not mummified.
Guests will come tonight, I'll be among them.
One after the other in every window branches of remorse keep opening.
Many words, pilgrims from lands of silence and the shadow of death.

The curtains flutter in the air, the doors turn on their hinges.

FROM *MOVEMENT TO TOUCH* (1968)

Holiday's End

He went off; didn't say when he'd be back
a short holiday, you might call it

But surely he'll soon be back
surely: that raven over a road which this once isn't empty
that caravan making its way through the Negev

He went off to die awhile
and then to rise from the dust, to come home from the desert

For his servitude is over, his sin is atoned for
in this endless silence

O, I know it by the disquiet in the air
which bears these conflicting rumors
(one of them is good)

I know it by the wind gusting over these dead words
these words which only moments ago knew nothing
I know it by this city which senses his loss.

You're No King

You're no king.
Your Ithaca's no sun, no marble.

You're no king
The mighty Homer doesn't follow you
Day and night
The whole long way.

And you've no sea.
You've no salt wind, no full sails.

You're no king
Under a crescent rounding to a full moon, on the way,
Among islands.

Still so much time.
Still a mass of sky.

You're no king.
You don't embark from the winter-teared shore.
You don't land on the summer-fruited shore.

You're no king.
You've no sea.

You've no ship for the awful wonders,
For a happy ending for your feet.

You're no king
You sit on stone. Silence.
Your fists are filled with your distance.

My Samsons

Look, my Samsons are coming back, the gates of Gaza on their
    shoulders;
smiling, they pass unseeing sentries.
Mint. Wind. Crickets.

Look, my Samsons are coming back, their Delilahs at their feet;
they move along my spine.
I'm awake.

Look, my Samsons are coming back, the memory of lions in their
    hands;
they march by in bare feet,
soundlessly in the unlit street.

Look, my Samsons are coming back, the frogs of the Vale of Sorek in
    their ears;
they make their way, they always make their way,
when was it I last lifted the gates?

Look, my Samsons are coming back, the slaughter of the feast in their
    teeth;

the wet ropes are torn, the riddles are solved,
my first grey hairs.

Look, my Samsons are coming back, no nails in their eyes;
they come back to me from Gath,
after the fire.

Look, my Samsons are coming back to the gloom of their nights
luminous with fox fire.

Of the Azazmeh Too

And of the Azazmeh* too, it would seem,
freckling the stony vastness
a shadowy intrusion into the realms of the sun

The Azazmeh, a stink of goats, camels, tar,
the women necklaced, veiled,
opened up in girlhood

A land of milk and honey and grain in seven kinds,
a land of mule and donkey cocks in summer heat

The sun, the whole sun, nothing but the sun
and fierce desert winds
and a life gone limp

And the bearded seers,
they of the torn feet,
their eyes divine embassies

And the cliff clawing at the sky
and the soul weeping its secret tears

*Azazmeh (also Azaazame): One of the Bedouin tribes, living chiefly in the Sinai Penin-
sula.—TRANS.

Pictures of Jews

to Ezra

My silent jailers, well experienced. Who love me.
Their look caresses my face to the very end.

I'm there.
Jail. Stones, iron, twilight.
They don't come to me now by inheritance.

I see them:
some of them alive, some lifeless,
free.
Simple smugglers, but shrewd
who know by heart the ways to heaven
and move in that direction, as to a land well known.
Their faces like the faces of weary sages.

And at times of frailty they come back
to a foreign land, to look and to ponder.
They come back like apartment renters.
And after a while their faces are blood.

And they move, they move and scatter in the wind,
the wind which wipes out all traces,
which carries the smell of the dead,
like a tired traveling salesman, black-white,
selling fear and trembling.
And his beard grows on the road,
and his house is distant, above and beyond the silence.

They come to me.
Their step is nearly noiseless,
it trembles like a sacred saving act. They come here.
They assault me, leaving a sad victory,
and quietly fall back within me to an ancient, distant royal town.

They come to me, from the plague,
across woods and fields and waters
from the tear which salted the sea.

And their faces the smile of sages,
over stones and metals and dark tar.
I dream them.

I'm not moving now.
Mesmerized, I maintain their movement
and they're murdered within me like fathers.
They're all alone.
Only God is with them.

Silk and Silence

You're so fragile.
You're afraid and at times like these you pretend.
You spend a long time combing your hair for my sake and for the
    evening.
The mirror returns the favor.
Your beauty measures the weight of these moments.
A dark mascara line extends your lids
And expires at a lonely rite of silk and silence.
The world is as small as you.
Your palm moves off. A small eternity.
The movement recurs, returns to fix the wayward hairs along your
    temples.
And now you're ready to come into night.

Piraeus

Free till eventide
free to look about—Piraeus
the sun waning over a dim
metallic sea

Lamps on piers and ships
open branches of light in the water,
officially the evening's begun here
earlier than expected

And later, to see these girls
one by one, two by two
mute terrible advertisement for paradise,

When the voices mount up out of silence
to fade again, so softly the very
water can be heard

And later, to see a ship that was at rest
putting out to the open sea
to be finally alone in the night
                    *
I've something else in mind,

something imagined in the evening air
reserved for me

Wait awhile, night will fall
night, forgiving night

Miraculously now the red moon rises,
a discarded stage prop
and sea winds come up to sweep the promenade

Later, I see people pacing the streets
and the pensive, sea-bemused statues

*

Later, as in a stately, languid dance
you wander the length of wet wharves
pacing streets
which do not hate you

You amble on
whiling the time away in painless reverie,
you move on
Columbus discovering shores already known

You move along the warm streets
like a stranger, like an addict,
full of good tidings

The blood bursts through the scorched
tunnels of your body,
struggling to bear the brackish tide

Northern Romance

I've gathered more data on a towered city
One like Edinburgh,

On basalt citadels
And the smell of burning charcoal.

I heard a soft light and twilight as long
As my yearnings for it.

I saw a plaster moon freeze
In a sky of gelid lakes.

I saw rusted guns
Guarding an ancient ballad
And fog coming in
Quietly cutting down the towers,
Denying the parks
Their permanence.

The radiant young women waiting in a dark city.
Purple dresses and golden hair.

Window-Dreaming with SAS

Dusk, first lights coming on,
Turreted town by grey lake, antique scene.
We've left behind the land of the wounded,
the land of mournful memories and Jews.
And dusk thickens over all these unbloodied waters,
and skinny Swedish girls troop by, blue-yellow evanescence,
headed for the lilac horizon. Dark, chill.
A beer and herring smell alongside a cannon
(it's forgotten the last time
it thundered at those Polish forts).
Skinny Swedish girls, a promise included in the price of the fog,
next to a turreted town gelid in its silence.
When were we ever here?
And what are these forests doing without us,
all by themselves?

In the Amorite City

In the Amorite city spared for my sake from the sword of Joshua
and the Lord of Hosts
on these scorched hills,
Her walls with their crumbling strength trapped in the conquerors' sky
unchanged, as they were, a remnant,
In the Amorite city whose gates gape before me in dreams

like the gates of a ghost city, slowly,
at the feet of dreaming ravens,
In the Amorite city awaiting me with bitter love
like her bitter smoke, her hardened dung, her goats in heat
on the stone paths to the gates,
In the Amorite city turning white for my sake on dim violet-drenched evenings
like a woman far off, remembering,
lighting lamps for my sake in blue-painted rooms,
to fend off black dreams
in the Amorite city
the scorched city which goes on loving me,
she whose men rest impaled alongside their donkeys
burdened for nothing with their legs up
she whose horses are effigies of flight
going on forever on every side,
In the Amorite city whose women wait for me forever
in mind-wrenching patience, strange brides
in torn windows.

flame and wood and blackened stones like these
who will move in these wretched fields

who will say cyclamen*
I say it again cyclamen
and he will ask for copper*

only five minutes of copper
on his way to Gavriela*
on his way to ravaged Gavriela

who will rest on the way

who will move like a silhouette on the hilltop
like some invincible angel
some angel moving on
asking for gold for the rest of the way

*Military code words: flowers are positions; metals, requests for artillery; women's names, destinations.—Trans.

sometime somewhere far away
the weeping will begin

An Age Is Ended

An age is ended, another kingdom's ended
in the dawn on these damned mountains,
in the fire that before your eyes has died away to cinder.

An age is ended, the other kingdom rises
before the soldiers, puffing cigarettes, who did not die before you
next to their comrades covered with grey blankets,
the stillness of the road.

An age is ended, another kingdom's ended
the birds healing on these cypresses
above the men tested and refined like silver.

An age is ended, the other kingdom rises
at the gate of these dying lions,

For an age is ended, another kingdom's ended
and by the tower all seems lost,
by the tower trading flag for flag.

For an age is ended, the other kingdom rises
next to the men resting in silence at its feet
atop stones whose value mounts from hour
to crazy hour.

FROM *GEḤAZI VISIONS* (1974)

And of all that was theirs only the letters were left
Still frequenting these hard dark stones,
Like legates from some other realm but not this place.
And so the line went on
On both sides these stones.
And I walked in the main street
Of a distant foreign city empty and elegant
Snow descending on my abraded face.
And even my footsteps covered by snow.

≈§≈

I live now in an ancient book.
I live now in the proper environment
which exports oranges and griefs
to half the world.

I live now in a white city
which burgeons with black dreams.
I live between rare imaginings
and absurd conditional sentences.

I move like a passing shadow
on a street unlike any other,
among hearts prepared for despondence,
toward the kingdom always to come.

I move between the saintly
and the lovesick.
I see men and women
back from the world to come.

              ❧❦❧

I'll be an amulet, I'll be good news
I'll stand endlessly patient
by doors importuned and respondent
and I'll deceive the monstrous deaths
like the love of sorcerers
I'll be the hand to lay on the pains
and at night I'll be a complaint department open and lit up
and I'll be almost
and I'll be your life hanging by a hair.

              ❧❦❧

I pray you, forgive me in the stillness of your shoes swollen
on these sands.
Grant me your silent forgiveness, brothers. Brothers in gloom.
And so I stand erect and watch over your faces,
in the spoken silence, the ever dwindling distance,
and with me my rescued soul.
I pray you, forgive me in the stillness of your shoes on these sands,
brothers in gloom.
I was a whisper. I spun vows about. I climbed the heights of prayer.
Still I'm no Elisha stretched out on top of you, I'm speechless
on these sands.
And so I stand in the west wind
beneath the southern sky so much at ease with it,
on this shrieking earth
my soul dismayed.
Watching over you. Until dark.
Until I'm called to move on westward and away from you,
still my hand draws near and touches flame and turns back once more.
Brothers. Brothers in gloom.

Nisan 5734
(Spring 1974)

FROM *TERRIBLE* (1979)

And This Happened

And this happened in Prague many years ago.
Through the wall I heard the lovers
Who for love's sake hadn't closed their eyes.

Through the window I saw a city dark and empty at 3:30.
A lone Skoda, nameless as a knife, roared out of sight.
Then nothing at all.

Only my sorcerer spirit, performing unseen wonders,
My spirit filled with what-if's.

Rain. Unheard. Barely seen alongside the stage-set street lamp,
At its base.
Czech placards hanging, gliding in the fading space,
Purple and blue.

Old Hebrew newspapers. Like a relative who's told his tale
And wept and paused
And now is silent at my side.

And there's no white hand to tap on my door, three taps.
There's no one to ask me the time
Or borrow a box of matches.

At the Train Station

And this happened in Prague many years ago, on a cold grey day,
On the bench in the train station, not far from the Old Town.

The locomotive puffed white smoke in the fog,
Reminding me of a trip I might take to a remote foreign town.

On the bench opposite sat a young woman in a raincoat.
She was wearing leather gloves the color of her purse.

She was a bit plumper than the ideal.
In her the blood of Slavs, a bell-tower provincial town and stormy skies.

I've never seen her before, he thought, I don't know her name,
But he knew he loved her.

Knew he'd rush to exchange the Bratislava ticket
If only she'd look up from the illustrated magazine and smile at him.

It happened in the fall of 1947, at the Masarik Station,
At dusk, as darkness fell.

Like French films about tiny hotels and train stations,
Whistles in the fog and rain, of course.

Album

The road to Eluela.
The road back.
The marathon dash to Eluela.
Her smile on the way back,
His steps,
His face still in her eyes.
Her flame in his hands.

All roads lead
To Eluela.
Her sheer brocaded gown.
Nights of frantic birds,
Dog nights.
The zodiac circling
In his eyes.

The fringe of his shirt
Trapped in her fingertips,
The blue sin
Of her signature.

The road that led to Eluela.
The road back,
Afterwards.

His face a reminder of Methuselah
Mesmerized
By the face of the princess.

Dance

Like a long step
There in slow tempo moving far off
And wave after wave like those days
It's a fogbound sea
And free
Like a long, terrible step of spare time
And open, almost sinful
And for nothing
And her face still hovering opposite mine
In the air
And it's so late
Don't go don't go let it still be blue and lilac and black and gold

Around me
Like this endless tango
Let it still be so

Thorns

One in ten, as the lot falls. So be it.
She comes in her only dress and nothing more. So be it.

I won't say not I, I won't go off when my name is called
I'll look and see the face of a wild beast. So be it.

No palace in the mist, no wall no towers in the forest heart.
A lone tree like a wanderer in scorched mountains. So be it.

A man arrives his face downcast, he has news for me once more:
Who promised you salvation and solace? So be it.

I saw a raven atop a mount of stones, he awoke and flew off.
And in my veins flows the blood of pauper kings. So be it.

Then I spent a night on a bed of stones, my head in the stars
And around me calm, as before a storm. So be it.

And the valley is filled with a mighty host, like Aram before me.
And between me and them no messenger of God. So be it.

Jericho

Jericho unknowing.
Long before they saw her in the dying light
She glittered, dreamily, in their sleep.
Her wall was their wall.

Inscriptions lack all trace of the doomsayers, moving among the palm
    trees,
Amid the purple crimson bougainvillea, to tell her something.
It does sound odd.
Such disasters don't unfold without some warning.

Rumors were rife about strangers, hairy, red-garbed from Edom,
Coming there, washing their feet in the cold streams.

A mighty city is heedless of such talk.

Only young whores, gouged by their virile iron
Till dawn rose in Moab,
Understood, confusedly, wearily, the fierce hunger.
They left an impression as forceful as the desert.

Jericho, gorgeous Jericho.
Jericho unknowing. No one put bits and pieces together
For a clear picture,
No one foresaw the blast of the rams' horns.
No one to piss, no wall,
Only dust.

If

If a flame has fallen among the cedars
What will the wall moss say?

If danger lies in wait for those who sleep
What will they say who watch in silence?

If the weary are dying to sit down
What will they say who go on standing up?

If in Oran plague has broken out
What will distant neighbors say?

If the hand is writing on the walls
What will they say who have the last laugh?

If even the innocent are scourged
What will they say who cling to God?

If the woman in love has wept into her pillow
What will the ancient ballads say?

If judgment pierces the mountains
What will the skeptics say?

If in the street darkness breathes
What will the glowing candles say?

YEHUDA AMICHAI

Born in the Bavarian town of Würzburg in 1924, Amichai came with his parents to Palestine in 1936. After a brief stay in Petaḥ Tikva, the family moved to Jerusalem, where Amichai still lives today. While yet in his teens, Amichai joined the British Army in 1942 and served in various units in the Middle East until 1946. He subsequently joined the Palmach and fought on the Negev front in Israel's War of Independence. After the war Amichai completed his studies in Bible and Hebrew Literature at the Hebrew University, and for the past thirty years he has taught at various schools and colleges in Jerusalem and abroad, among them the Greenberg Institute, the Hebrew University, the University of California at Berkeley, and New York University.

His orthodox Jewish upbringing and education, his knowledge of German and English, and his extensive war experience have been the main shaping forces in his poems and other literary works. His poetry is infused with familiar phrases—usually in ironic usage—from the Hebrew liturgy and Bible; it evokes the tropes and diction of Rilke, Auden, and Günter Grass; it resounds with the harsh oddities of warfare and the confounding need continually to discover meaning—or despondence—in the process of everyday living.

One of the most distinctive elements of his poetry is its disarming, deceptive simplicity. Amichai's poems often read like a personal diary, a record of someone's random musings. This impression is attributable to several central characteristics of the poetry: the quasi-autobiographical voice Amichai often uses; the aphoristic nature of many lines; the patently casual, candid tone; and the creation of sequence through ostensibly unconnected images and metaphors.

Two figures predominate in much of the poetry: the child and the lover. Both create a tone of intimacy and innocence, both evoke a resonance of sentimentality, an imagined security along with an obviously vulnerable naïveté. These images are clearly figurations of all the world's true believers who hope so innocently for uninterrupted happiness and goodness. They struggle inevitably with the intransigence of time and change, with the ambiguous but intractable order of being. Exhibiting both a lingering despair and a healthy appreciation of paradox, Amichai celebrates humanity's futile yet often amusing attempts to survive through intimacy and sensibility. People are really like children lost in the world; as manifestly mature beings in control of their existence, they at best make only dubious progress.

Through the fifties and sixties Amichai's popularity could be attributed to his combining various themes, voices, and images with issues dominant in contemporary Israeli life, mainly war and soldiering and their effects on the Israeli psyche. Much of the poetry of those years expresses his sense of the painful gap between notions of national heroism and the need for personal equanimity. Amichai handles the dual tension with masterful mixtures of compassion and wit, tragic irony and spirited humor. The soldier, though dedicated to his role of protector, is yet much like the child and the lover; he himself is so much in need of security and protection.

Though he has for the most part avoided literary journalism and politics, Amichai became for a time the heir apparent of Natan Alterman, who throughout the forties had published droll political poems with catchy puns and tongue-in-cheek references to contemporary events that helped the Israeli populace through some of its darkest hours. The satiric tone, the playful language, and the blend of traditional and colloquial Hebrew diction are to be found in Amichai's poetry as well. His emphasis, however, is more personal, the central voice an apolitical one that muses unceasingly on everyday experience: ordering food in a restaurant, riding a bus, coming home on leave, traveling to strange places, making love on the seashore, visiting the Western Wall.

Beyond his deft juxtaposition of archaic and contemporary diction, Amichai's stylistic forte is his skillful use of figurative language. The characteristic "simplicity" of his poetry is largely due to his similes, which often have a homey, down-to-earth ring. With impressive original force he has turned aside Alterman's symbolist tendency (and Shlonsky's formal metrical patterns as well) and opted for more concrete linguistic structures and more prosaic rhythms. Another major technique he uses is a chainlike series of seemingly disparate metaphors that actually links the poem's parts into a unity of meaning. It may be said, in view of this artistic ploy (patterned after Rilke but given its own stamp by Amichai), that many of Amichai's poems develop in burgeoning blocks of figurative patterns, rather than in direct, vertical lines.

In the seventies and early eighties Amichai seems to have become more private, pensive, and sensual in his writing, not casually or playfully, but rather in a way that suggests a hungering for self-insulation, an uncontainable need for immediacy and privacy. The poems of this period have a far less figurative style; the rhythms are much more akin to casual speech; "live" voices speaking in brief, poignant phrases emerge from within nostalgic scenes or sentimental reflections. The mood is, for the most part, dejected, the voice engulfed in sadness. Feelings of loss, aging, and nostalgia prevail.

In its broadest context, Amichai's poetry, like some of Auden's, displays a blend of sardonic wit, an overriding tone of dejection, and a heightened sense of individual and historical transitoriness. His impish disdain for sacred cows and formal rules, his casual but potent images of inconsistent realities, his penchant for ironic portraits of innocents and intimates, his unfailing response to national trauma—these qualities have made Amichai one of Israel's most enduring poets.

FROM *POEMS 1948–1962* (1962)

God Has Mercy on Kindergarten Children

God has mercy on kindergarten children,
less so on schoolchildren.
And for adults he has no mercy at all,
he leaves them alone
and at times they must crawl on all fours
in the burning sand,
to get to the aid station
and they're gushing blood.

Perhaps for true lovers
He'd have mercy and pity and shade
like a tree over someone asleep on the bench
in a public park.

Perhaps even we should hand over to them
the last coins of kindness
our mother bequeathed us,
so that their happiness will protect us
now and in other days.

My Father

The memory of my father is wrapped in white paper
like slices of bread for a day's work.

Like a magician who pulls rabbits and towers from his hat,
he pulled from his small body—love.

The rivers of his hands
poured into his good deeds.

Look, Thoughts and Dreams

Look, thoughts and dreams weave over us,
warp and woof, a camouflage net,
and reconnaissance planes and God
will never know
what we really want
and what our destination.

Only the voice that rises at the end of a question
still rises above the things and hangs suspended
while artillery shells turn it into
a tattered flag,
a shattered cloud.

Look, we too proceed like
the flower, in reverse:
Starting with the blossom rejoicing at the light,
descending with the stalk, ever more weighty,
reaching into the closed earth, waiting there a while,
ending like a root, in the darkness, in the womb.

Lovers in Fall

The radio broadcast the news—
but we felt old, very old,
and we left home after filling it with
our warm lives, like a pot steaming with food—
and fall was on its way.
The embassy flags told us where the wind was coming from,
and without knowing it we had lots of time,
like a clock that tells time's passing to others
but doesn't know it itself.
And people passing by saw us and said:
Falls are coming, we've grown, the children are older—
then they'd use us to measure the bounds of their happiness.

And this year, too, we've seen how the clouds
intrude in the same old way
and how we, each year, each day, each hour,
come by another way.

And now fall has come.
And the embassy flags billow with longing for their lands
and they're far away from our worries below,
and the sailors of our blood's raveled ropes call
out their confusing cries, and we don't know if
it's "land ho!" or "squall ahead!"

And now it's fall.
And majority wills weigh on us like heavy clouds,
and unlike migrating birds,
we must wait for the warmth to come to us,
to be in us and not in the lands of refuge.
And unlike the dead
we must find our well-deserved rest
in each other,
deep in safe chambers
like the pupils of our eyes.

Instructions for the Waitress

Don't take the cups and dishes
away. Don't wipe the stains
from the tablecloth. It's good to know:
others have been here before me.

I buy shoes that someone else tried on.
My friend has a mind of his own.
My love is another man's wife.
My nights are sleeping with dreams.
My window's painted with raindrops.
My book has someone else's comments in the margin.
The plans for my new house have
strange people by the door.
My pillow shows the contour of
a head that's not there.

So don't take the cups and dishes
away. It's good to know:
others have been here before me.

The Onus of Mercy

Count them.
You can count them. They're
not like sand on the seashore. They're
not like stars without number. They're
like separate people.
On the corner and in the street.

Count them. Look at them
watching the sky through ruins.
Leave the rubble and come back. Where can you
come back to? But count them, for they
soothe their days with dreams
and walk about freely, and their unbandaged hopes
are agape, and that's how they'll die.

Count them.
They learned too soon to read the terrible
writing on the wall. To read and to write on
other walls. And the feast goes on in silence.

Count them. Be there, for they've
used up all the blood and still need more.
Like major surgery, when you're weary
and sorely wounded. For who's to judge and what is judgment
unless it's the full import of night
and the full onus of mercy.

FROM *NOW IN THE STORM* (1968)

From "Jerusalem 1967"

1

This year I traveled far
to see the silence of my city.
A baby's soothed by rocking, a city's soothed by distance.
I lived in longing. I played the game of
Judah Halevi's four weighty blocks:
My heart. I. East. West.

I heard bells ringing in the faiths of the time,
but the wail I heard within me
was always of my Judean desert.

Now that I'm back, I scream again.
And at night the stars rise like the bubbles of drowning men,
each day I scream the scream of a baby being born
from the chaos of houses and from all this great light.

3

Light on the Tower of David, light on the Church of St. Mary,
Light on the fathers asleep in the Cave of Machpela, light
on the face from within, light on the luminous
honeycakes, light on the clock and light on the time
that passes through your thighs as you take off your dress.

Light light. Light on the cheeks of my childhood,
light on the stones that wanted the light
and on those that wanted to sleep in the darkness of squares.

Light on the fence spiders and the church cobwebs
and the acrobat stairs. But most of all, upon them all
is the light of the terrible, truthful X-ray,
in letters of bones, in white and in lightning: *mene
mene tekel upharsin.*

Quick and Bitter

The end was quick and bitter.
But the time between us was slow and sweet.
Slow and sweet were the nights my hands
did not touch each other in despair, but,
in love, touched your body, which came between them.
And when I came into you, it was
the only time joy could be measured so
precisely by sharp pain. Quick and bitter.

The nights were slow and sweet,
but our now is bitter. It grates like sand—
"Let's be sensible," and other such curses.

And the farther we stray from loving
the more talking we have to do:
words, words, and long, ordered phrases.
Had we stayed together,
we could have become the quiet.

In My Time, at Your Place

We were together in my time and at your place.
You offered the place and I the time.
Quiet and freckled, your body lingered as seasons changed,
as styles slid over it, short or long,
patterned or silk, white or tight.

We turned human values into animal codes,
quiet and freckled and everlasting.
Still we were ready to burst into flame any moment
along with the dry grass of late summer.

I shared the days with you. Nights.
We exchanged glances with the rain.
We weren't much for dreaming;
we weren't even in our own dreams.
And in this disquiet the quiet nestled
and slept. In my time, at your place.

No doubt the number of dreams
I'm dreaming of you these nights
foretells the end of us,
just as a flock of seagulls
the imminent sighting of shore.

Patriotic Reflections

You: caught in the net of the chosen
people's Homeland. A Cossack fur hat on your head.
Heiress to their violence. "And it shall come to pass."
Always.

Take your face: angular eyes, you and your
Chmelnitsky* eyes, the high cheekbones of
a marauder hetman, and a Hasidic
dance of celebration.
Nude on stone at twilight
by the water canopies of Ein Gedi.
Your eyes shut, your body open, like hair.
And it shall come to pass. "Always."

We: caught in the net of the Homeland
speaking now in this tired old tongue,
a tongue torn from its biblical repose. It
wanders blindly from mouth to mouth. A
tongue that once described miracles and God
now says car, bomb, God.

The square letters want to stay
closed, each letter a closed-up house.
To stay locked in a final mem,
to sleep in it without end.

*Bogdan Chmelnitsky (also Chmielnicki) (1595–1657), leader of the Cossack and peasant uprising against Polish rule in the Ukraine in 1648, which resulted in the destruction of hundreds of Jewish communities.—TRANS.

I Am a Live Man

I am a live man,
the son of a dead father,
the father of a living son,
with many plans for growth and decay
much like the seasons.

I hear the somewhat raspy voice
of this full life,
smell the perfumed smells
which rise up to do me in.
And on these Passover days I eat
lying down, perhaps to die,
put my watch on the table before me,
in memory of your face. The brittle matzah breaks
so easily between the fingers of my hands. The door
moves so slightly this miraculous midnight
and the hair of my lust stands on end once again
in these days as well.

We Will Live Forever

We will live forever.
The earth will weigh its fruits
with yesterday's dead and the vine will adorn
the gaping quarry in its dying. Who sings now
at the ripening of the lonely, at the hardness of rock, at the seasons.
The perfect form of fruit is asked of them,
the harshness of a smile in a night of love. And their escape
is no escape, and their happiness
shatters all the vows of those in gloom, and a great
excuse will shield them as well.

We will live forever.
The kingdom of the deceived will not fall,
even if we know the reason for trees, the cause of thorns
and water, the season's soul, the purpose
of sins and the numbers of those who die of lust.
Everything bears the stamp of stone. Or perhaps:

fervent hair, a picture of a strange wedding,
an inherited veil, a moonstruck bride walking
in an empty circle, smiling, the childhood of smiles.
Or maybe: mountains. The thoughts of a wandering God.
And the beloved's heart like the mouth of a trumpet, suddenly
from the darkness. Or the opposite: my heart lies
on my drying body like a flopping fish,
singing with a twisted mouth, forced to sing so as not to choke on dry
    land.

Or possibly: My window and I, a window widened
becomes a door, my entry's another floor
in the houses, my families have grown, we will live forever.

Wait for me at the Crusader ruins. There was some
sort of plan, a defense of what decayed
long ago. Wait for me there this evening
with your body already dark and the hair of your lust
still lit up, reddish, absorbing
the last bits of sunlight. We will live
forever.

Elegy

The wind won't come to draw smiles in dream sand.
The wind will be strong.
And the people walk without flowers,
unlike their children at harvest-time feasts.
And some win, but most are beaten;
they pass through the arch of other people's triumph
and like the Arch of Titus everything appears in relief,
the warm beloved bed, the loyal polished pot,
and the candelabra, not the one with seven branches, but the simple
    one,
the good one that was never disappointing, even on winter nights,
and the table, the house beast, standing silent on its four legs . . .
And they're brought to arenas to fight the wild beasts,
and they see the heads of the crowd in the coliseum,
and their strength is like their children's crying,
unceasing, unceasing and useless.

And in their back pocket letters rustle,
and the winners put words in their mouth,
and if they sing, it's not their own song,
and the winners fill them with great longings
like loaves of bread dough,
and they bake them with their love
and not they but the winners eat the warm bread.

But some of their love stays with them
like plain designs on ancient clay vessels:
the initial, modest line of feeling, around the edge,
then a spiral of dreams,
then two parallel lines,
mutual love,
or a likeness of blossoms, in memory of
childhood's tall stems
and thin legs.

Now in the Storm

Now, in the storm before the calm,
I can tell you things I
couldn't in the calm before the storm,
for we'd have been overheard and found out.

That we were only neighbors in the breeze,
thrown together in an ancient Babylonian khamsin.
And the later prophets of my arterial realm
prophesied into the firmament of your flesh.

And the weather was good for us and our hearts,
and in us the sun's muscles grew strong and golden,
an Olympiad of feeling with thousands of spectators,
so that we'd know and stay on,
so that there'd be clouds again.

You see, we met in a well-defended spot, at the
point where history began; a quiet place,
free of hurried events.
And the voice began telling its story that evening,
by the children's bed.

And now, it's too soon for archaeology and
too late to change what's already done.
Summer will come, and the sound of hard
sandal steps will go on sinking into
the soft sand
forever.

FROM *NOT JUST TO REMEMBER* (1971)

Jews in the Land of Israel

We forget where we came from. Our Jewish
exile names expose us and bring on
memories of flowers and fruit, medieval cities,
metals, knights turned to stone, dozens of roses,
spices that have lost their aroma, precious stones,
lots of red, lines of work that have since disappeared.
(The workers are gone, too.)

It's circumcision that does it.
Like the Bible story of Shechem and Jacob's sons.
It hurts all our lives.

What are we doing here, coming back with this pain.
The longings have dried up with the swamps,
the desert is flowering and our children are lovely.
Even pieces of ships that sank on the way
have reached these shores,
even the winds are here. Not all the sails.

What are we doing
in this dark land that casts
yellow shadows slashing our eyes.
(Sometimes you hear someone say, even after forty
or fifty years: "The sun is killing me.")

What are we doing with these mist souls, with the names,
with forest eyes, with our lovely children,
with our quickened blood?

Shed blood is not tree roots,
but it's the closest to them
that we can come.

Testimonies

1

It was like silver, like an ending.
It hurt.

The yellow flower's fragrance a reminder of desert.
There were three. The face of one
the face of an eagle. The second was called
away somewhere
and left.

2

They met among trees.
They cast their love and shadow on the ground
and stayed standing.
They pointed there
and said: There's
where the Dead Sea must be. There's
the place of our death.

Behind them were sad beasts
one next to the other.

Her thighs were wide and conclusive.
Her head final.

The forehead familiar.

3

Or a tree testimony about people.
They were two.
They sat beneath me,
they lay down.
Afterwards I never saw them again.

May our father's virtue cover them, or
some other large robe.

From "Achziv"

1

Clouds have come up from the south, the Nile's
overflowing its banks. There's hope then.
War pretends it's peace here,
this beach still believes everything,
the floating pieces of paper and all their writings,
the algae, the seaweed, the gestures of strange and distant
peoples whose heirs are the waves.
The rock in the water is covered with moss
and is warm as a body under damp wool,
a man carrying a tune strapped to his shoulder.
Tall girls legs like the ruins
of lovely homes with high arches.
A seabreeze cools my lusting groin,
I touch the sand's skin,
I touch the sea's muscles,
the shadow shattered in the ruins but not torn,
a snake severed by a piece of glass
hangs from the wall like the beautiful belt
of a woman undressing, on a stone threshold,
whose house is in ruin, a melon is murdered and splattered
and a weightless face is lifted
from the heavy tears slowly descending.

4

Time after time you're placed at the imagined
starting line, like chess pieces for a new game,
you're tired. You give yourself
a used toy, wrapped in pretty paper,
received without surprise, without cries of joy.

Sailboats and horses have turned into playthings,
Palmach songs are still sometimes played at weddings
among aunts and boisterous beggars.
The sea is silent and big, and your look,
turned toward the distance like a searchlight,
meets in its long journey the woman sitting next to you
and turns her face toward the lighted distances
without the hope of closeness again.

5

And this is how it begins now, my late
soul, perhaps the last, to grow on me
on the outside, like a climbing vine on a house
about to be abandoned, a decoration for the ruins.
And still there is hope. The clouds still
come in the middle of summer
and a young woman's brought along
her heart like a big red ball to play with,
the sea still uses her suntanned skin
for his falling tears, for his foamy laugh.

What can one put up against all these?
My slow walk, not even love;
my walk is the fifth season that never changes.
My face covers itself with the wind so it won't break,
from above come echoes of super-night sounds
and grey hair is the hair of return.

FROM *BEHIND ALL THIS HIDES GREAT HAPPINESS* (1974)

From "Songs of the Land of Zion Jerusalem"*

4

I have nothing to say about the war
I have nothing to add, I'm ashamed.

I forgo all knowledge I've absorbed
in my life, like a desert that forgoes water.
I'm forgetting names that I never thought
I would forget.

And because of the war I say once again
for the final, simple sweetness of it all:
The sun revolves around the earth, yes.
The earth is flat as a piece of lost lumber that flowers, yes.
There is a God in heaven, yes.

37

All these stones, all this sadness, all
the light, scraps of night hours, ashes of noon,
all this twisted pipeline of sanctity,
the wall and towers and rusted halos,
all the prophecies that could not wait like old men,
all the sweaty wings of angels.
All the stinking candles, all this synthetic tourism,
feces of salvation, joy and genitals,
refuse of nothingness, bombs and time,
all the dust, all these bones
on the way to resurrection and the wind,

*"The Land of Zion Jerusalem" is the last line of Israel's national anthem, "Hatikvah" (Hope).—TRANS.

all this love, all
these stones, all this sadness.

Take them and fill the valleys around,
so that Jerusalem will be flat
for my sweet plane
to come and carry me off.

38

And in spite of it all I must
love Jerusalem and remember
what befell her at the bridge of Gethsemane,
that its death was a watershed
between memory and memory, between hope and hope,
that it was the land and the fruit of the land
that in it a lulav and trumpets and wings of angels
were bound together in one bond, that
all the salvations and deaths and consolations were
for the sake of heaven and for the sake of the land,
that it rose and stood firm that it stood and fell
and its body is another gate in the wall
and its voice a throng like the throng of resurrected dead,
that for sword is for sword, that
for night is for night, that for clamor is for quiet.

Stirred by the breathing of a small, sleeping child
he rises now and opens wide with supernal joy
and all of Jerusalem is the explanation for his death.

From "Laments on the War Dead"

6

Is all this sorrow? I don't know,
I stood in the cemetery dressed
in the camouflage clothing of a live man, brown
pants and a shirt yellow as the sun.

Graveyards are cheap and unassuming.
Even the wastebaskets are too small to hold

the thin paper that wrapped the store-bought flowers.
Graveyards are disciplined, mannered things.
"I'll never forget you," reads
a small brick tablet in French,
I don't know who it is who won't forget
who's more unknown than the one who's dead.

Is all this sorrow? I think
so. "Be consoled in building the land." How
long can we build the land,
to gain in the terrible, three-sided
game of building, consolation, and death?
Yes, all this is sorrow. But
leave a little love always lit,
like the nightlight in a sleeping infant's room,
not that he knows what light is
and where it comes from, but it gives him
a bit of security and some silent love.

FROM *TIME* (1977)

3

Tonight I think again
of many days that sacrificed
for one night of love.
Of the waste and the fruit of the waste,
of plenty and of fire.
And how painlessly—time.

I've seen roads leading from
another man to another woman.
I've seen lives defaced
like a letter in the rain.
I've seen tables with things left on them
and wine with the "The Brothers" label
and how painlessly—time.

41

Evening lies along the horizon and gives blood.
Flocks of birds arise like black mist.

Love is a reservoir of kindness and pleasure,
like silos and pools during a siege.

A child sits alone in its bed,
its kingdom is a kingdom everlasting.

People put fences around their houses
so their hopes will not be in vain.

Inside a white and closed room, a woman
decides to grow her hair long again.

The earth is turned over to receive the seed.
A secret army post rises up in the dark.

66

Late in my life I come to you
filtered through many doors and diminished by stairs.
There's nearly nothing left of me.

And you, a surprised kind of woman, living at half strength,
a wild woman with glasses, the elegant bridle of your eyes.

"Things love to get lost and be found again
by others; only people love
to find themselves." So you said.

Later you split your full face
into two profiles, one for the distance
and one as a souvenir for me, and you were gone.

DAN PAGIS

 Dan Pagis, born in 1930 at Radautz in Rumanian Bukovina, was raised in Vienna. A survivor of the Nazi concentration camps, he came to Israel and lived for a while in Kibbutz Merhavia. After teaching for several years at the regional kibbutz school in Qiryat Gat, he enrolled at the Hebrew University in Jerusalem and supported himself as a high school teacher of Hebrew literature. The holder of a doctorate in medieval Hebrew poetry, Pagis has been on the faculty of the Hebrew University since the early 1960s and has published several scholarly works, among them *The Secular Poetry and Poetics of Moses Ibn Ezra and His Generation* (1970) and *Innovation and Tradition in Secular Medieval Hebrew Poetry* (1976).

Much of Pagis's early poetry exhibits the word plays, allusions, and verbal virtuosity of the medieval Hebrew poetry with which he is so familiar. To these linguistic qualities Pagis has added much wit and a wry charm, which link him to his modern mentors, Shlonsky and Alterman. Shlonsky's short, poignant nature lyrics especially have left their mark on Pagis's work, but Pagis has developed his own voice, mainly with a playful inventiveness and controlled use of sound, ambiguity, and irony.

The poetry offers a variety of themes and concerns: the unbridled passage of time, the weight of unwanted memories, the abortive fruits of the scientific revolution, the unresolvable horrors of the Holocaust. Most of all, Pagis presents himself as a multidimensional observer of the human condition and psyche. With a tone of clever perceptiveness he explores the inner life of trees, seashells, animals, spaceships, dead soldiers, and crossword puzzles. Often the objective is simply to highlight the poet's fertile imagination, the intellectual acumen and sense of humor he brings to bear in discovering the hidden possibilities in everyday natural phenomena. Just as often, however, the aim is more philosophical, psychological, or moral: to show how empty society and culture have become, despite the progress of modern technology. These ironic implications permeate much of Pagis's poetic work.

In *Shadowdial* (1959) and *Late Stay* (1964), Pagis continually conveys a sense of human entrapment in time and memory. Passive verb forms, especially the passive participle, emphasize this inescapable condition. The *Late Stay* poems, with their themes of sudden awakening and heightened awareness, stress the psychological dilemma inherent in this static experience. Loneliness, alienation, self-doubt, the inconclusiveness of being, the irresolution of past traumas—the central themes reveal a more personal perspective, one rich in awareness of human psychology. The style here is proselike, the structure narrative and fluent, the tone aphoristic. The observer is more humanistic, emotive, philosophical. The irony is emphatic, for many of the poems have a dualistic structure: the first half sets the scene, delineates the situation; the second conveys a sobering reversal or discovery that negates or redefines the actual condition. The endings are often poignant punch lines, connoting the unavoidable recurrence of things, the paradox of a progressive inertia. We always seem to be running in place, says Pagis, continually finding ourselves back at the start.

In two later collections, *Transformation* (1970) and *Brain* (1975), Pagis reverts to his poetic role as a wry perceiver of contemporary events. The butt of his sardonic odes is the world of technology, especially the accomplishments of space-age explorations. Here Pagis becomes a cultural commentator, humorously aspersing scientific progress as an enroachment on civilization rather than its evolutionary vanguard. At the center of these collections, however, are two significant developments: his first explicit poems on the Holocaust, and an intensive, epistemological inquiry into the nature of the mind and imagination. Burdened by the unshakable memories of his own Holocaust experience, Pagis expresses the victims' shock in poems with purposely elliptical endings; he agonizes in disbelief and guilt as an accidental survivor, a reluctant witness, an unworthy rememberer and transmitter of inexpressible scenes.

In his latest collection, *Double Exposure* (1982), Pagis has continued to create his witty observations of everyday objects and events. He adds new dimensions to his work with poems on American scenes, mainly New York City, a long, purposely archaicized work on war ("Siege"), and several experimental, short prose-poems. In their totality, Pagis's poems of inner perception not only display the author's keen intellectual bent but also imply a view of poetry itself as intelligence.

FROM *LATE STAY* (1964)

Epilogue to Robinson Crusoe

From an island teeming with parrots
and devoid of speech he came back,
as if he'd just been waiting
for a good wind to come up.
He's returned: here he stands.
But suddenly all the years turn back
at the door.
         And then,
among the hollow armchairs, he knew
what had happened; he grew wise
as one who knows there's no going back.
Too wise to live on, vacant and greyed, he lived
with the pipe of his stories, and he talked—
to silence the ticking and chiming
of his dead—he talked and talked
of an island abandoned by time.

Honi*

When he returned and opened his eyes and stood there, uncalled for
at the highway's edge, wrinkled up in his old coat,
he remembered and knew the night and was no stranger:
As always, the clouds, stealing across borders, hurried by,
and a blind rain, begging at doors, tapped
on its tin for a penny,

---

*A sage and miracle worker of the first century B.C., known as "the Circle-Drawer." According to legend he slept for seventy years (like Rip van Winkle) and, when he woke up, found none of his family or friends alive.—TRANS.

and a city of passers-by revolved
in glass lights as if in some other darkness.
And so, brought back by God, he dreams on.
The year's not so urgent; he's no longer late.
He can still ascend to the circle that opens on high
and go back to sleep,
forgotten amid the Milky Way.

Logbook

While the wind upon the waters still returns
to whoever bestowed it, and the flag is
lowered from the mast, and a muffled
mutiny smoulders down below—we knew at last:
the maps had lied, and light as cork
we were caught in their net and floated on
as if we'd set sail.
How did we come upon this treasure island? From the depths
rise lovely pearls of air as from a drowning man
and in the open skull-box we can see
diamonds of salt. There's nothing to do but
kneel on the deck and give thanks
to heaven and the sleepy sea that gave us strength;
for we, who hadn't yet sailed, had arrived.
One must cast anchor and forget.

꿍

A witness anew, I'm bound to pass on
through the day's electricity, hurrying through rain
amid discords of wires—another street, always just for now—
and then inside, to a grey-love movie, whose heroes
have died long ago before the empty, seat-gaping
house, before the house of shadows.

A witness anew, ascending the last subway,
quiet at night, toward a suburb at the back of

a two-faced city. Branches which
thrust their shadow into the mist,
an alley I avoided,
a twisted iron gate I did not enter.

Had I stayed, who would have saved me
from the fists of my heart? A stranger with collar raised
in the November wind,
caught in the thick of my veins, with someone
even later than I, aligning his steps
with mine, at each and every stop
before hate. This is my lot. I'm bound to pass on.

A Letter

The tracks diverge from each other. I don't know
what might happen yet in years past,
what the next moment has already forgone
in the rail car behind. Countries recede from me;
at times while traveling
I remember a sleepy window, waving its shade,
or a sudden wall hurled up
from the night.
How could I
write to you, my beloved old photos:
the borders are fixed, they've held me back
from line to line. But
don't worry about me. By my side my reflection
grows old in the black windowpane.

Needless Return

After it all the hunchbacked village remained
beyond the years of death, along with night,
recalling me only vaguely.
The sleepless dogs

still tell the same lies from dusk to dusk,
the tin rooster
on the weather vane's cross still pretends
to give me direction.
I won't go astray, I've no need to ask:
the address is etched on my flesh; why should I struggle,
I can't grasp myself. By mistake I've come back
and found out: everything happened by design.
Relentless, I'm condemned to go on.
It's nearly daylight, soon they'll see me alive.
Why did I bring my eyes with me
back from the abyss.

Decline of an Empire

In the sea at Ashkelon stand the amphoras of Rome,
weighty generals with great reputations and paunches,
who went off to a clever war of conquest
and sailed for the south.
But the day was hot and languid, and they settled
on a land of light and water, where silence
was everyone's concern, and refused to take charge
of the masses of fish or the slippery populace.
And so they resigned
and marked their freedom on their bodies
with a seal of seashells.
In colonies of algae and coral
and in nonchalant sands they still stand
on their right to rest
and not want any more.

Ararat

While all the ark's survivors lurched onto land
and in joyful disarray
chattered and roared and shouted for prey

and howled for procreation
and overhead came the rainbow and said
no such end would happen again—the end did come
for the carefree fish that had lived
off the mishap like smooth speculators.
Now, on stiffening soil,
they were caught, their fins disheveled,
and with mouths gaping wide,
they died, drowning in air.

Plans

Amid the dawn's scaffolding, lines of ink and lead,
I must open and rise up, unwilling,
from the fisted earth,
unplanned, craving
fire from water, like unslaked lime.
And before I knew my strength
the electric nests awoke, new flashes,
antennas receiving the new year,
and the voices of people to come
hidden in inner rooms of air—and high
are the flights of clouds. Already a city; and I, captive
on an overturned hill,
resign myself. I've lived. I've been given rest.

FROM *TRANSFORMATION* (1970)

Testimony

No no: of course they
were human: uniforms, boots.
How to explain it. They were created in the image.

I was a shadow.
I had a different maker.

And He in His mercy left nothing in me to die.
And I fled to Him, rising so light, blue,
appeased, I'd say: apologetic:
smoke to omnipotent smoke
that has no body or form.

Another Testimony

You are the first, and You remain the last,
if You're not able to judge between plea and plea,
between blood and blood,
listen to my heart, hardened in judgment, see my plight:
Michael, Gabriel,
Your angel collaborators,
stand and admit
that You said: Let us make Man,
and they said Amen.

Pages of an Album

Destined for greatness, he lies on his stomach, a pacifier
securely before him. Expanses of floor await him:
All target, impossible to miss. And then
he's grown up, photographed on his feet, forgetting
what he'd never learn. For a moment
he steps into his class picture and smiles
up on top, by the teachers. Meanwhile,
with a woman or two at the beach, footsteps
fading in the sand. At the same time he rests,
adult and yellowed, in a pensive pose,
hand to forehead, dusk. Even before he's resolved it, he continues
cautiously down a gloomy corridor, like a thief,
and at the end finds
himself waiting for him in the mirror:
The light, too strong,
of the flash
captures
his image
and darkens
the glass lenses
of his eyes.

I Was Before I Was

I was before I was, who now
in a startled night wind
must turn back
weary in the dry grass—
in thrall to a troubling voice.
The candles glow with mortal grace
at the crossroad; they've instructed me
to come: home, a strange name which
lies in wait for me within these veins of darkness.
Locked between my blood and my blood,
a blind fever folded within me
struggling to emerge from the sweet emptiness,
struggling to shriek all at once

in the air which rushes through my lungs.
I no longer am
—I was a distant summer—and now
must bear the sight of another light. I am
who I am. I cannot recall anymore.

Final Exam

If I'm not mistaken:
It's the lightning that's expired
which only now flashes in
the eye.
It's the air at the amputated hand
which causes
the pain.
            —No, not so. That's not the place of remembrance.
            You've spoken only metaphorically.
            But you, my servant, you
            must be precise. I expected more from you.
            But it's all right, my servant, fear not,
            You will not fail.
            Think it over. Ponder it once more then answer me:
            Where is remembrance?
            Whose flash was it?
            What has been cut away?

FROM *BRAIN* (1975)

Autobiography

I died with the first blow and was buried
in the rocky field.
The raven taught my parents
what to do with me.

My family's respected, largely due to me.
My brother invented murder,
my parents, tears,
I, silence.

Later the really famous things happened.
Our inventions were refined. One thing led to another,
orders were issued. Some even killed their own way,
cried their own way.

I'll name no names
out of concern for the reader,
for at first the details might be frightful,
but in the end they're tiresome:

You can die once, twice, even seven times,
but not ten thousand times.
I can.
My underground cells reach everywhere.

When Cain began spreading over the earth
I began spreading in the womb of the earth,
and my strength has long surpassed his.
His legions are leaving him and joining me,
though it's only a sour revenge.

The Limits of Physics

In the soft armchair sprawls the boy unmoving.
The world obeys its laws.
November, scattered graphite, moves on,
turns yellow in a cloud, glimmers
with a challenge of sulfur.

In the armchair sprawls the boy.
On his head, unmoving, waits the lightning rod.
The brass shines bright.
In the magnetic field scurry metal shavings,
rising, in a slight slant, to their fate.
The boy sprawls unmoving in the magnetic field.

Now the cloud turns white. The brass telescope
(also called the spyglass)
captures it with ease.
The world obeys its laws with a dry rustle
like falling leaves (but softer).
Cold electricity sparkles like this
when amber's rubbed with silk.

In all these are very great comforts, but
suddenly, at a cloud's parting,
a whirl of swallows
bursts forth
from a whirl of swallows.

The boy's alive,
he's alive, he bursts forth,
he lifts himself from himself.
All the laws obey him at once:
his fall's
a free fall.

Armchairs

The slowest beasts are the
soft leather armchairs with large ears
in the living room.

They multiply in the shade of a potted philodendron
or a dark ficus.
And even though they're happy to live
more slowly than elephants,
they're constantly leaving on
secret safaris
to infinity.

Biped

The biped is quite a strange creature:
in bodily form he's related
to the other predatory animals, but only he
cooks animals, only he seasons them,
only he wears animals, even as shoes.
Only he thinks
that he's a stranger in the world, only he protests
his fate, only he laughs,
and what's more amazing, only he,
of his own free will, rides a motorcycle.
He has twenty fingers,
two ears,
a hundred hearts.

FROM *DOUBLE EXPOSURE* (1982)

November '73

You speak in a very ancient tongue.
Of a month ago. Dead. Forgotten.
All vows of the words of then
Are null and void.
You're at pains to fulfill them:
Against your will
You take the names in vain.

A body whose dust has been burnt,
A body whose number is obliterated.
You sit down, an innocent,
To call them all by name.
Against your will
You take the names in vain.

This name list
Do you still call it: They?
The letter just delivered
Do you still call it: You?
Names, names in vain.

Siege

1

The hidden monastery garden, poppies, drowsy noontime.
Aside from myself there's only one person here in the sun.
Who is it, why it's my neighbor, the well-known dust contractor.
I'm glad we met, he says from inside his skull, but for the moment
Excuse me, I'm in a rush. We're digging in. Later we'll have time to chat.

2

Suddenly the hoopoe. Suddenly motionless.
A tuft of feathers motionless. The edge of a fence.
The torn eye a black mirror
For the soul from there.
Suddenly it takes flight: to the pine
Beyond the wall.
The moment's created out of nothing, swallowed up into nothing.
The pine is empty.

3

First burial was in the dust,
The track of legions.
A second burial, of gathered bones, was
A secret ossuary carved in limestone.
Now, at the close of some century, in the scorch of noon,
The ossuary is empty.
A third burial is in the wind.

4

We have time, the mosaic and I.
I was born under the sign of Libra.
And it under the whole zodiac.
Everything's included in it. All the signs.
We have time. Both of us, slowly, have disintegrated.
The tiles, torn loose, are scattered,
Free of fate, ready
For the game of chance.
Here's a tile: smooth, intact,
Every surface empty.
I pick it up, a die,
Aim at the mosaic's center,
Make a bet, throw it down:
Zero: I win.

5

Red to black. Wild protest of poppies
Quietly scatters, falls. The seeds
Trapped, lie in hiding.

And meanwhile summer, young tyrant,
Brings up for battle the globe thistle's spines.
The forces are even. Soon
Bare feet in the field. Soon
The inevitable: scorpion.

6

Between stone columns, at the gate,
Something turns white, flickers,
Whose signals,
Whose flag of surrender?
An old newspaper, this morning's, hugging the wall,
Sneaks off, is caught and taken captive.
Front-page headlines are carved
In the limestone.

7

From the monastery tower
The antenna-cross broadcasts
The news at noon, first the headlines:
Third burial is in the wind.
The fertile dirt returns, covering the land.
Second burial was in the limestone.
Nearby, a stone's throw away, stands
The city, a carved sarcophagus.
First burial was in the dirt.

8

And so the armies have dug in. The front is jagged.
If I stray right or left
I'll step on a skull. The area's mined.

9

I see: The forces are even.
Who'll attack first, who'll surprise whom?
From the blind spot on the slope I hear
A labored shift of gears:
The present comes up from the plain,

A pincer-movement bypass:
The siege is tightened.

10

I report: The equipment's in good order.
Ten years or twenty
After I fell in our victorious fight with Titus
Someone came, perhaps my orphan,
And reverently gathered up my bones
(As it is said: A day of rejoicing),
Arranged them nicely in the sarcophagus,
Little ones and big ones separately, and at the top, the skull.
He covered it, sealed the emergency supply,
Disguised the equipment as dirt, and since then
Constant readiness.
In this emergency the equipment is ready,
The order confirmed:
I gather myself up, straighten my bones,
Put on sinews and skin, full dress,
And report to my regiment
Right now, in the end of days.

Notes [by the poet]

1. The poppy *papaver somniferum* is used to produce opium, which eases pain and makes one forget. Part 1 in the original is in classical hexameter, as are several tombstone inscriptions in the Land of Israel of the Second Temple period and later.

3. At first they would bury them in pits. Once the flesh had decayed, they would gather up the bones and bury them in ossuaries. That day would be a day of mourning, and the next, a day of rejoicing, which is to say that their ancestors protected them from divine wrath. (Palestinian Talmud, Mo'ed Katan 1, 5.)

10. Rabbi Meir said: One gathers up the bones of his father and mother, for it is a day of rejoicing. (Mishna, Mo'ed Katan 1, 5.)

If they find the body with its limbs scattered, they may not consider it complete until they find the skull and most of the rest. Rabbi Judah said: The spine and the skull may be considered most of the rest. (Tractate Semahot 2, 12.)

Unclassified. Upon receiving orders, report for duty at your unit's assigned position. You must bring with you all the military equipment you have in your possession.

Then the land will surely give back the dead which it receives today for safe-keeping, and nothing at all will change their look. (Baruch 5, 2.)

Houses

At the edge of the page the pen
Quivers, a seismograph, and tries
With thin, sharp-angled lines to sketch
The shaking of the floor.

The shaking intensifies. The angles sharpen.
But this instrument has become obsolete,
It doesn't sketch even the edge of the truth
That the table is smashed to smithereens,
The house sags,
The earth gapes beneath it.

In the ensuing silence, amidst ruins,
The pen is released from all its obligations.
It scribbles whatever it likes on the page,
Nonchalantly connects angle to angle,
Joins all the threads in the middle,
A masterplan
For a spider's house.

Tropical Greenhouse

Simulated Eden,
clever cage of cultivation.

Glass walls pretend they're air African
rubber fans drip calla
gape from all sides ficus intertwined the moths
lured by magenta by the Devil's Orchid
a thousand tongues reach out to dark nectar.

Far from these,
way out,
in an arid field,
concealed by the color of flesh,
erect, thin,
blossoms
Youme,
a mediterranean hermaphrodite,

Youme,
A unique species.

Photo at the Bridge

In sun and snow slumbers
This otherworldly Brooklyn
Between soft, strong
Sabbath cushions.

Before me, high up, the bridge is suspended
With slender, ice-clear threads, suspended motionless.
From here to the horizon moves
Only my mouth's vapor.

No need for haste. On the coastline the inscription:
DEAD END.
It has a number of readings
All quite literal.

Seventy years I'm at the end of the bridge
With a heavy box camera on a tripod.
My hands, beneath the black cloth, wait for
The right light.

As if it's still that Jewish snow.
The brilliance is blinding,
Overexposed.
The photo will show only
A white frame.

And this is no metaphor,
Just as I'm
Finally leaving for home. Behind me
Prances a joyful greywhite line, seagulls
Of Lubavitcher Hasidim.* They wave a greeting
And pass by in the snow, like me.

---

*Members of the Hasidic sect (also called Ḥabad) whose spiritual leaders, the Schneerson family, originated in the village of Lubavitch, near Mohilev, White Russia. Their center is now the Crown Heights section of Brooklyn.—TRANS.

Words

After a long summer of silence comes this windblown morning: Now I'll be able to speak again. I open the window—and right away wind grabs at me, snatches the words from my mouth as always.

But this morning I'm stubborn and insist on every last word. I regret only what I left unspoken.

Outside the Line

Lines of a poem, long, short: each joined to the end decreed for it. Outside the line we fly in space, return, burst into flame at the edge of air, burn up, scatter darkness around us.

The Souvenir

The city where I was born, Radautz in Bukovina, cast me out when I was ten. That very day she forgot me, like someone dead, and I forgot her, too. We both felt comfortable with that.

Yesterday, forty years later, she sent me a souvenir. Like a troublesome cousin who demands affection just because of blood ties. She sent me a new photograph. Her most recent winter portrait. A canopied wagon is waiting in the courtyard. The horse is turning its head, looking fondly at the old man locking a gate. So it's a funeral. Two members are left in the Burial Society: the gravedigger and the horse.

But the funeral is grand: All around, in a whirlwind, crowd thousands of snowflakes, each a star with its own crystalline design. Still the same urge to be special, still the same illusions. For all snow stars have a similar shape: six points, a Star of David, really. In a minute they'll all melt, run together, a larger mass, just snow. Within them my aged city has prepared my grave as well.

Acrobatics

The first drum roll—and he's a coil of air, limbs in all directions, he whirls, descends in a great arch, lands on the tip of his finger. Nice, but we've seen it.

The second drum roll—and he's a ball floating among seven balls, pushing and pushed, descends in a great arch, catches them all on his nose. Nice, but we've seen it.

Suddenly, with no preparation, all at once, his legs stand on the stage floor, above them his pelvis, his stomach, his chest, his shoulders, his neck, and beyond it his face turned peacefully toward the dark. This is the height of art.

NATAN
ZACH

 Natan Zach was born in Berlin in 1930 and arrived
in Israel in 1935. He studied at the Hebrew Uni-
versity and began publishing poetry in the early fif-
ties, especially in the new journal *Likrat*, which
he edited with Benjamin Hrushovski. In the mid- to
late fifties, Zach was active in the founding of the
journal *Akhshav* (Now), and later, in 1961, coedited another new journal,
Yokhani. Throughout much of the 1970s Zach lived in England, where he
completed a D.Phil. in English Literature and later taught at the Univer-
sity of Essex. Most of the works in the *North-by-Northeast* collection
(1979) were written during this sojourn.

Zach's works mark a distinctive breakthrough in the development
of Israeli poetry. His search for a nonsymbolic, nonallusive mode of po-
etic expression prompted a declaration of all-out war on the Shlonsky-
Alterman hegemony in Israeli letters. Centered on the founding of *Likrat*,
the literary rebellion fought to shed what its followers considered the
outdated cultural baggage of remote, obscure, stylized, highly structured,
sentimental, biblically allusive, ideological modes of writing. Zach was
the movement's mentor, its guru and primary spokesman.

Embodying an overriding desire for openness and experimentation,
the new writing led Israeli poetry away from its devoted adherence to
Russian-modeled poetic structure and the lyricism of French symbolism.
The young poets—among them Ory Bernstein, Moshe Dor, David Avi-

dan, Aryeh Sivan, Dan Pagis, Dahlia Ravikovitch, and Zach—turned to the modern British and American poets and to contemporary European modernist styles. T. S. Eliot, Pound, Yeats, Marianne Moore, E. E. Cummings, Allen Ginsberg, Rilke, Else Lasker-Schüler—these poets, among others, became the new sources of poetic inspiration. Their collective novelty, if not all of their individual idiosyncrasies, created new possibilities of poetry for Zach's generation.

Zach's own poetry abounds in variety and virtuosity of genres, themes, voices, and techniques. His most significant collection, *Different Poems* (1960), includes biblical poems, dream poems, poems on poetry, philosophical poems, narrative poems, short lyrics, poems on the death of the poet, dialogue poems, dramatic poems, and a mock oratorio. Themes proliferate as well: the inescapability of things, an awareness of life's changelessness, a preoccupation with death, an attitude of world-weariness, the transience of relationships, the questioning of one's actual imprint on life. Essentially pessimistic in tone, the poetry in great measure is playful—a combination that creates an aura of the absurd, mirroring the probable influence of T. S. Eliot. The poet's only solace, it seems, beyond his own wittiness, is the act of poetry itself, the creative force that creates words to express humanity's fundamentally tragic fate. Even poetry, however, is amorphous, powerless; it is merely "something" that shows evidence of the poet's existence, of some human endeavor.

Of the myriad techniques found in Zach's works, the most innovative and impelling is his use of dramatic immediacy. In many poems, the speaking voice recalls or is immersed in a dramatic situation that is entirely ambiguous. The reader is taken into a "live" situation, the nature of which cannot easily be determined. Indeed, the purposeful ambiguity serves to heighten the immediacy that the reader confronts. Often, too, the poem moves rapidly from one situation to another, adding a confusion of scenes, voices, and personae to the already apparent uncertainty. Instead of sequences of metaphors (like those in Amichai's poems), Zach presents close-knit sequences of dramatic events that challenge the reader to discover common denominators of meaning. This sort of ambiguous, dramatic tableau—Zach's enduring trademark—both embodies his anti-symbolist style of writing and demonstrates his view of poetry as mainly an emotive, psychological experience, not solely an intellectual exercise.

The use of dramatic immediacy and its accompanying ambiguity reflect fully the revisionist perspective Zach has attempted to express through his poetry. (Ironically, Natan Alterman, the symbolist poet who was the target of Zach's revisionism, may have been an unconscious source of these techniques.) In his recurring motifs, too, Zach may be seen expressing his revisionist role. Nearly all the motifs—the sea, the wind, birds, mountains, islands, falling leaves, clouds, trees, night, the moon, ships, seasons, sky—are stock romantic images. Irony, however, is the point; for in most cases these images are set in antiromantic contexts. Though they momentarily hold out the possibility of lyrical appeal, of edification, these images ultimately—and ironically—convey loneliness, hopelessness, death. Even images of lovers or of women, though promising security, intimacy, and quietude, usually come to express the wish for such idyllic conditions rather than their actual attainability.

The use of colloquial Hebrew—with an occasional archaism for emphasis or tone—also sets Zach apart from his more classically oriented predecessors. The poetic language of Shlonsky and Alterman, with its embedded allusiveness, evinced a cultural-linguistic virtuosity that blended the pastiche of biblical speech with the poems' dramatic connotations. Zach virtually stripped his poetry of this semantic weightedness. His linguistic allusions tend to be overwrought, hence playful and satiric. His literary allusions also move away from biblical frameworks. Although he has a number of effective psychological and sardonic biblical poems (mostly about tragic figures like Saul, Absalom, and Samson), Zach, with the aim again of broadening Hebrew poetic horizons, turns for his subjects to world literature and to non-Jewish fictive or mythic personae (Robinson Crusoe, Desdemona, Orpheus, Midas).

Humor and sarcastic wit also play major roles in Zach's work. A plethora of overbearing, sardonic rhymes, double-talk puns, limerick-like verses, repetitious litanies, mocking streams of highbrow phrases, folkloristic depictions of talking animals and dying toys—these feats of imagination entertain as they lull the reader into a false euphoria. For in essence what Zach creates is a poetry of disdain. His main contribution, his ultimate overturn of the tradition, is the displacement of a poetic discourse of national, ideological issues by a poetic voice of private feelings and individual fate. While he argues aesthetically for closer contact with life's common experiences, Zach expresses in the body of his work a basic recognition of death as the most personal, most pressing reality.

FROM *DIFFERENT POEMS* (1960)

How the Days Passed. Who

1

How the days passed. Who'd have believed they'd
pass this way. How did the time pass and the sky
and the wind?

The wind raged in the tree, spurned our memories.
You who were mine no longer
belong even to the stars.

2

Beneath the covering of leaves the fall
secretly, locust-like, awaits its turn:
Slowly slowly, not all at once, the gross flesh falls away,
the terrible hair
withers.

Deadwood on the seashore
draws comfort from the wind.

The fish flit off with a ripple of content.
Forever young, their eyeballs made of hard water.

The place to be set aside for us in one of those places
one of these days
is ready:
The earth, laid open, is never heedless.

I can hear the horsemen charge
over the prairie. Mother! Mother! screamed the boy, I can see
their horses' hooves. Sleep now, sleep, the helpless mother said.

My son whom I bore, my son whom I brought into the world
sees nothing.

When will the wondrous diamonds sprout—
the very coal itself. When will I see you again and when
will I hold you endlessly, my lips
whispering love.

I don't know. To be more precise: I don't know.
What was mine I tried to give. It's a
long and tiresome story. This isn't the place to tell it.
It hasn't changed the world.
The salt within me speaks.

3

He doesn't know
and never knew, they told the investigator.
Now that he's revealed
everything he knows,
how clear it is he doesn't know,
how clear it is he tells no lies.
I know, the investigator said,
There are things I know,
there are things I remember.
That's how I am. I can't be otherwise.

Max Is Dead

1

Max is dead and his sons
are left behind in want of bread.
The rain falls slowly in these regions,
the leaves, too, fall slowly.

The wolf has twelve faces, the wary farmer said
locking the shed.
The poet made some final changes
in his draft,

then clicked the safety closed.
What's safe is safe. In the drawer

the wind turned pages and read
the adventures of Romeo and Juliet in the war

they'd never go
back to
once it was over.

2

I recall the place,
I was bold enough to say,
and also the faces I loved,
but that was my boyhood.

Don't think it's silly,
said the friend.
Please don't think it's silly.

3

But I love my wife and children,
the prisoner said in the downpour
as he was led
over the empty heights.

Again there's no need for it,
replied the monk carefully scrutinizing
the manacles on his hands and feet.

It's not far from here,
the guide explained.

Savages once inhabited these hills.
By now they've fled inland away from the shore.
The storms you see, the white froth of the waves—
this is what the sea does to them.

He said no more. I felt a slight choking in my throat.
I too once walked this road.

But I'd better shut up. I can't get through to them.
The wind that raises the dust and leaves it to our sons
in the shape of death remembers nothing.

The prisoner's a frail creature. His body coming apart—
a white stork in a blind light.

Don't rush, said the guide, don't rush. Why
worry someone will get there before you.

War Confession

I've grown distant from my grandfather
under the piano.
I no longer wait
for him to say something,
to hear my name while he sings.
It seemed to me he'd already forgotten
but it turns out it was I who forgot.

Sometimes I'd ask the pilots
to bring me my rations, the K rations,
straight to the shelter where I was hiding.
I don't see myself believing in foreign gods.
Anyway I went unanswered. The war passed over my head.
They didn't know the way, they said there was no air corridor.

I don't smoke American cigarettes, not even
before sleep. I don't fly in airplanes.
I'm not that naïve.

He vanished in the fog. They say his
fuel ran out. There's no sense looking into
what's done with. Unless, of course, the family inquires.
Metal fatigue, was the reason given. In the matter-fatigued cities
naphthalene laments move about
in bright-hued darkness
like an alchemist's laboratory.
The proper gentleman of my age
counts worn coins
which have no history, no hope of redemption.
Uncovered layer by layer,
late dust in the eyes of an old, relentless look.
With trembling hands the antiquary unfolds
the family tree long since discredited. In the light of an untheatrical sun
the hairy hands are huge. The monsters, on the other hand, are
  microbes

magnified by water. The mountains are only
places from which to descend. Airplanes are bees
no longer buzzing. Instead of honey they gather bombs
with hands instead of wings, liable to dust and sleep. Deceit lights
beacons on the mountaintops to signal another conclusion. Scoundrels
    of oblivion
debate, point with balding heads to maps which even yesterday
had nothing to conceal under the sand.

Harvest Month

Harvest month. A full moon
Rounds out the pain of earth.
A gleam of springtide floats
To the verge of shadow and falls.
Evening. Like evening now in a land
Breathing crows' poison, thinking of
Lovers on a night which darkness stars, raising a cypress
With strange longings. A man's song in his blood cells, the thought
He thinks in his image, waking with evening
To his name like death
Embedded in his body like
Heat in rumpled pillows.

Samson's Hair

I've never really understood Samson's hair:
its immense secrecy, its Nazirite mystery,
the prohibition (perfectly understandable) against talking about it,
the constant fear of loss of locks, the endless dread
of Delilah's light caress.

But I have no trouble at all with Absalom's hair.
Obviously it's beautiful, like the sun at high noon, like a red vengeance
    moon.

Its fragrance is sweeter than the perfumes of women.
Conniving cold Ahithophel can't bear to look

when he sees before him the reason for David's love:
It's the most glorious hair in the realm, the perfect motive
for every uprising and afterwards the terebinth.

The Painter Paints

The painter paints, the storyteller tells his story, the sculptor sculpts
the poet, however, doesn't poetize,
he's a mountain by the roadside,
or a tree, or a scent,
something in flight,
or already passed, something that was
but won't be again, like the seasons,
heat, cold, ice, the heart's
laughter when it loves,
or water, something immense, mysterious
like wind, or a ship, or a poem,
something which leaves behind
something.

Give Me What the Tree Has

Give me what the tree has and what it won't lose
and give me the power to lose what the tree has.
The faint tracings the wind makes in the darkness of a summer night
and the darkness which has neither trace nor shape.
Give me the shapes I once had and have no more
the strength to think that they've been lost. Give me
an eye stronger than what it sees and a hand
harder than what it seeks. Let me inherit
you without receiving anything that's not past
the moment I receive it. Give me the power to come near,
without fear, precisely to what I'm not meant
to hold dear, let me come near.

I Hear Something Falling

I hear something falling, said the wind.
It's nothing, it's only the wind, said the mother soothingly.

Both of you are guilty, declared the judge to the defendant
A man's but a man,
explained the doctor to the anguished relatives.

But why, why, the boy asked himself,
disbelieving his own eyes.

Whoever doesn't live in the valley lives on the heights,
the teacher had no trouble solving
problems of geography.

But only the wind which knocked down the apple knew
what the mother had concealed from her son:

that never, never, would he find any comfort, none.

Like Sand

When God in the Bible makes a promise,
he points to the stars.
Abraham leaves his tent at night
and sees lovers.
Like sand on the seashore, God says,
and man believes it. Even though he knows
"like sand" is only a figure of speech.
Since then sand and stars remain tangled
in the web of human metaphor. And maybe it's senseless
to speak here of men. They weren't spoken of just then.

Look, it says explicitly "like sand," and this must mean
the ability to suffer. Or do you think that nothing
was forbidden then and there's no longer—explicitly no longer—any
    limit.

Like sand on the seashore. Look, there's not a word there about water.
And it explicitly says "seed." But such is Heaven's way
and maybe Nature's way as well.

Prologue to a Poem

This poem is a poem about people:
What they think and what they want
And what they think they want
Besides this there's not much in the world
We ought to care about. And it's a poem about human deeds,
Because the deeds are more important
Than the things that aren't done. And every man wants
His deeds to be remembered long after the things
Left undone are forgotten.
And it's also a poem about a grand and spacious land
And when the darkness descends, wrapped in sunset
Like pity, a man might
Mistake it for a desert and so it's obviously also a poem
About a desert and about human beings crossing hot sand which moves
In their blood and it's a poem about people everywhere: How
They feel when the blue night sings the song of caravans
And how they taste sand in the charred fuselage which falls and sings
Like a burning love note: Instead of prose, this is a poem
About houses torn down and others put up in their place
But different from those which came before: Poets will sing
Of houses as long as there are poets in the world, but maybe
Not as long as there are houses. And finally, these are poems
About war and were written in the heat of battle and at a writing desk
    and without hope.

Death Came for Michael Rockinghorse

Death came for Michael Rockinghorse early one morning
but Michael Rockinghorse wasn't quite ready
to go with him. Come with me, Michael Rockinghorse, said Death
to him, but Michael Rockinghorse rode up into the mountains
and down into the valleys.

The sun had long since risen and lit up the surrounding
ruins. From horizon to horizon you could see no sign
of life. Come with me, said Death to Michael Rockinghorse.

Fishermen were out on the shore busily fixing their nets. Loop
within loop. Fat fish lay on the sand in the playful sunshine.

Heat lay heavy on the shreds of night
like stone on seaweed.

Come with me, Michael Rockinghorse, said Death. In the excavations
one could see heads cracked like nuts. Water dripped on the rock
like pins in living flesh.

Come with me, said Bitter Death, eyes tearful as he burst into song:

Michael Rockinghorse, Michael Rockinghorse.
Some people hunger while others ponder,
some people sink while others flounder,
come with me, Michael Rockinghorse,
together we will wander.

*And this handsome horse, this beloved horse Michael, burst into answering
song:*

Witlessly the train travels,
witlessly the girl loves,
witlessly God hovers above.

But Death persisted:

Michael Rockinghorse.
Far off on the shore
there's water in great supply.
Come now, I'll take you straight up to the sky.
I know a simple charm.
Michael Rockinghorse, I mean you no harm.

And the chorus goes on with its rhythmic song:

In the bottle there's a lot of water.
Many hands have touched the letter.
There's a line in the office but no redeemer.
Michael Rockinghorse, don't be a dreamer.

And Death repeats:

I loved her well, I loved her true
And thus the two of us were two.
Now that she's gone I'm forlorn I'm blue.
May Heaven take pity on me, too.

And the poet is compelled to add something of his own:

There are pictures in the album and a corner in the heart
With an angle and a melody.

And all the angels echo with a mad religious shriek:

There are pictures in the album and there's a corner in the heart
with an angle and a melody.

Michael Rockinghorse, Michael Rockinghorse,
How confused, you can see, Death now seems to be.

And Michael Rockinghorse bursts into an awful neigh of sadness when he
realizes he can't change what's been done:

I was here, it's as clear as shadow.
No one cares what I had to say.
All my errors others will follow.
Into the mountains—who'll follow my way.

And since the episode of Jephthah's daughter has been hinted at the poet says:

If the father's cruel, it's Jephthah's daughter who's to blame.
Jepthah's daughter, it's her shame,
Michael Rockinghorse, that is so.
Shadow is your greatest lover,
Michael Rockinghorse, you should know.

And since he knows his heart is torn in two he makes a few remarks:

Softly. Softly. Softly. Softly.
Softly (surprising) the menorah burns.
In the corner, corner, corner, corner
the deadly poison waits its turn.
Woman, if you've seen what you've seen what you've seen what you've
     seen—
no earthly remedy will cure your spleen.

And this handsome horse, ah this beloved horse Michael follows Death so
slowly with lowered head.
And Death walks along before him, as women soothsayers rush up from the
side:

Tell her. What are you waiting for?
A fleeting shadow are your days. What on earth are you waiting for?
The flower from the tree is born. But ice remains of the heart forlorn.
Tell her. What are you waiting for?
Tell the story of the handsome horse.
Tell the story of Michael Rockinghorse.
And how shadow, alas, was his ultimate course.

FROM *NORTH-BY-NORTHEAST* (1979)

In the Course of Time

In the course of time the original
plan goes awry.

What was carved in rock is erased again
as if the lines and contour returned to stone.

Marble rusts in the water, the color of the brick
is spoiled, everything liquefies, is washed away.

In the canal where only branches
float a shoe sinks.

Stars of wood stream on the transom,
the house's profile bends like a tree, bends more in water.

What was cut in sharp angles long ago
curves and twists again.

Like ripples and nets in the waves, a movement
of wave against wave with the wind and wave above wave

With a passing boat. Everything that's built upon the sea
yearns to become water again and flow. A window

Casts a transient strip of colored dye into water
in nature's flow. Opening a window is hazardous.

There's no rock which doesn't have its day and no day
which hasn't burned in the rock like sediment
growing like algae, like seaweed.

A Soft Warm Breeze

A soft warm breeze and the summer land awakes,
and camels in the street dust, a swarm of bees
borne in the smoke. Scions of Canaan
still fill the streets.

The splash of ebb tide, rock-splitting waters
deepens the depth of the well, in the book
Rachel still approaches, the moon rises
and gnaws holes in the dark.

The blood's ancient madness
still stones people alive. And a heavy hand extends
a wet cloth to soothe the brow,
to promise the patient in the bed

That he'll surely feel better tonight.
There's something to say for promises,
in our heart's desires is cast
a distant secret no one can interpret.

The wadi which wends its way,
the city which rose upon salt,
Job's bizarre end—
bear witness to an inevitable future.

The Problem

The problem, of course, is to form a shape
like a diamond, but also like a wide bed
where you can stretch out your limbs
without banging your head on the wall
and like a taut string
with no dusty corners.

What we're destined to say
we say with dubious fluency;
what one wants to say
is often said between the lines;
but what one strives to say
remains unsaid, as if destined.

And again this evening the sky's a vast inert space
and planes and clouds draw lines, curved, delicate lines:
they're the dynamic principle, what's written and erased.
And fall incites in you the complaining fruit
which asks only to stop, to slow down, to hold back
each color at the black gullet of approaching night.
This is impossible; there is no time.

A poet's time is always too long or too short, like a shoe,
narrow and tight or stretched beyond use.
Whatever you have to say to the next generation
must be said right now, but you're
still busy with the scraps in the drawer
and that may be best: last year's rain
won't be remembered by anyone but you
and what you have to say to your grandchildren
won't be returned to you for review or proofing.
Here you need cunning: That's the static principle.
To speak to the moment like a newspaperman
and to hope it will go on for a while
or as long as it can.

FROM *ANTI-ERASURE* (1984)

Nameless

A beautiful city, infected, like a sore
A spot of light upon the water. The destroyer's entry,
It always destroys. Like an elegant scalpel.

This is how the living are kept from the shriveled, hard flesh,
The mother's flesh from a child's scorched corpse in a burnt-up car.
A difficult time? It's always difficult.

Native city, residence, homeland, even then just words.
At the Sternheim Café they danced a generation too late:
It was clearly impossible to dance backwards.

Arnold Zweig in slippers,
ZVAIEG in Hebrew on the mailbox,
This ZVAIEG* won't make any flowers.

"To my dear, unforgettable friends,"
Friends and not friends,
Forgotten and not forgotten.

Also coming home from his day's work was the former capitalist, a
    construction worker;
Arbeit macht das Leben süss.
The Jewish Pyramid† collapsed, and he fell off the roof.

Since then he's limped. But there still was hope.
Where there's life there's
Hope

Ahasver,‡ a middle-class Wandering
Jew, suddenly poor, with a wife and child and no furniture
    (repossessed):
Zionism is always nourished by cataclysm.

*"Zweig" in German means "twig." The name was scrawled incorrectly in Hebrew on the
mailbox.—TRANS.
†A Zionist catchword for social normalization.—TRANS.
‡One of the names of the mythic "Wandering Jew."—TRANS.

All this wasn't so terrible: Herz committed suicide,
The doctor, in the temple, with anatomical precision:
For this he passed his exams and hit the bull's-eye

But it was still possible to live.
It was a matter of luck, too: Over there
It was much worse.

Wien Wien nur du allein.
Frankfurt am Main.
Berlin West.

Kohn, the judge, sold rabbits
And sausage in a bag that looked like a schoolboy's.
He also went back to school.

Lolleck, his son,
Paid the price. In full.

Dollfuss and Schuschnigg, where are you?
Who will wipe the dust from your eyes
And for what.

À la guerre comme à la guerre.

Envision this: a distant picture.
I see a woman in her kitchen, she looks familiar
I have a feeling she's close by

And suddenly distant. And hot and cold. Stop! Stop!
It's me knocking at the door, it's me,
At least tell me your name, my name.
It's me, you see.

No she won't tell, she's busy.
That's the way dreams are, they don't speak,
It's all symbols, interpretation, but there's no one to interpret.

At least say one word.
Tell me, is death good? Is there peace?
Is it easier for you there? No more pain?

Broken as a dish, the voice grows weak
A distant echo comes back, Speak, speak
But not a sound, only the words I seek.

A wounded city, torn, leprous

Beautiful city, are you silent, too?
You too have nothing to say?

The problem was one of love.
All the rest we could have overcome.

A Poem Too Late

It was distant, as usual, drops still on the windowpane
That night, as you said, as I said,
And we were close to agreement, but very
Distant in everything else.
Men don't talk about it. Men don't tell.

Three times the winter has come and gone, clues everywhere:
Every dish I handle drops and breaks.
Is it the spirit, is it the body
Beset by a sudden spasm, has it let go?
Men don't talk about it. Men don't tell.

Her hair was reddish-black, the color's blended in,
A certain tenderness remains, a small streak of tenderness
And maybe not tenderness. It's hard to be precise about these things.
It's hard to explain why it's hard to be precise.
Men don't talk about it. Men don't tell.

I said tenderness, I could have said more,
Something can always be added after the fact.
One bulb of the two in the room has burnt out,
One's not enough for reading, but it's enough for crying.
Will I cry on the balcony, on the chair, on my bed?
Men don't talk about it. Men don't tell.

Against Sadness

When even a turning to memory
Is suspect: even wrinkles are known to have lied:
What of this is skin itself

And what is by extension: a regional tan
Or an adjustment to the sun, what
Of the mask is a mirror and what

The everyday game, when all other games
Have gone sour and the poem's not quite right,
Not yet in shape.

Above all happiness demands precision.
Don't be happy before it's time
But when it's time, be happy without apprehension.

Sorrow, fear and other painful symptoms
Are too oppressive: a world unto itself
Leaves no room

For talking with a neighbor, for ironing,
For a blackbird, for a lover's frustrations,
The usual complications.

Sadness is mass communication,
A small screen which dwarfs large shapes,
A large stage where nothing happens.

Nature colors everything with natural colors:
Even happiness in black and white
Can be real.

That explains the need for chance, to preserve
At least an illusion of something more lively
Than the usual: That's what happened, at the time

I hardly knew it. Like a photographer: The lens
Was dirty, a hair got in the way,
Here's the hair, the dirt.

For if we're destined to live in this
Trap of then and now, when all the rest
Is merely empty middle, intermission at a movie—

We must at least fill it with sounds,
Movement, laughter, speech heard
Even when there are no words, in the pause,

To abstain from facile beginnings
With nothing beyond them
And from finished products

Which are followed—like a motion picture—by another product,
Without making the difficulty a rite.
But "It's been terribly difficult" is correct:

The difficulty is terrible enough.

DAVID
AVIDAN

Avidan's is a poetry of iconoclasm, confrontation, overstatement, and experimentation. His methods are mainly a rhetoric of bombast, a structure of random association, a sarcastic use of parody—characteristics that identify Avidan with the various avant-garde movements of modernism: Russian futurism, French surrealism, expressionism, and the "beat generation." His mentors are Shlonsky (in his younger, Mayakovskian phase), T. S. Eliot, and Allen Ginsberg; there are also affinities, mostly stylistic, with U. Z. Greenberg, Natan Zach, and e. e. cummings.

Born in Tel Aviv in 1934, David Avidan studied at the Hebrew University in the early fifties and began publishing his poetry at that time. From the start he aligned himself with the *Akhshav* group of writers and has remained close to them throughout his career. In the 1970s, when the journal was revived, Avidan became one of its coeditors. Aside from the nine volumes of poetry he has published to date, Avidan has been active in television and theater, as well as in the graphic arts, with several solo and group exhibitions in Israel, Europe, and the United States. He has produced his own short films and has translated extensively from his own poetry.

The world view reflected in Avidan's works is that modern civilization is generally maddening and essentially dehumanizing. Social and cultural narrowness, deception, snobbism, and opposition to change are repeated offenses; war, in particular, is identified as a thoroughly obsessive, wasteful experience. The central issue, however, is existential: the endless repetitiveness and cyclicality of things, a seemingly cosmic control of human destiny. Aging and death are the only certainties. Avidan's tone is world-weary, despondent, fatalistic; the speaker seeks "a comfortable, undisturbed place to scream in." The antidote for the frustrating, unrelenting fixedness is poetry itself: poetry alone provides "huge expanses of spiritual freedom"; poetry alone offers a reliable way of emotional release; poetry alone serves as a route to immortality.

Avidan understands poetry as power. Blending existentialism with a pervasive iconoclasm, his voice is emphatic in its sarcasm; it turns hostile—at times virulently so—and lashes out at social conventions, at middle-class manners and values. His voice attacks the "compelling forces" of normal living and invokes a personal "initiative" system to combat them. The poetry increasingly takes on a cynicism, self-centeredness, and hyperbole of the American "beat" poets. "I'm a Jewish bum," Avidan's paraphrase of the beatnik motto, sets the rejectionist tone. The appeal is to the young and energetic, to risk-takers, to a readership of intellectuals and mystics possessed of "the body-boldness and vigor of rock-group audiences." Speaking directly to the reader in a kind of person-to-person monologue, the voice singles out the hero as Humbert Humbert, Lolita's lover, who knows the shock of reality will overtake him but boldly risks the nonconformist act. Eventually—and ironically—even poetry is attacked as a "dismal-traditional-frustration of words-upon-words," a useless exercise in cultural conformity.

Avidan's way of overcoming this ultimate frustration is to project continually a poetic method of innovation and experimentation. Thus, he boasts a number of firsts: the first Israeli poet to communicate poetically with a computer; the first to produce pornographic films; the first to write under the influence of LSD. In short, he is as a poet constantly at the forefront of new technological and experimental opportunities, all in the name of advancing poetic possibilities. Embodying this spirit of artistic inventiveness—clear echoes of surrealism and futurism—Avidan's works of the late sixties and seventies express an insistent egocentrism. Initially a pose of unconventionality and self-reliance, the attitude seems to border on the narcissistic: the poet, with his instinctive sensibility and intellectual prowess, occupies the crossroads of effective communication; he possesses the superhuman ability to bring world peace in a flash; he epitomizes the modern savant, whose multiple "Thirtieth Century" agencies are catalysts for the new age of human and scientific discovery. "In this great cosmic democracy," Avidan writes in large, bold type toward the end of *Messages from a Spy Satellite* (1978), "everyone can be God."

Accompanying the blatant narcissism is Avidan's primary stylistic technique of random or free association. The poet, he notes, listens to "the ancient language of signs" and sets down the messages in writing. He calls himself a "thought-choreographer," assembling a collection of random notations made over a number of years. An aesthetic self-consciousness, so pervasive in his work, is an adjunct to the unconventional stylistics. A great deal of energy and space are devoted to explaining the poetic processes, especially when the product is deemed particularly inventive. In such instances—the best example is the long introduction to *Personal Report on an LSD Trip* (1968)—the diction is elevated to such levels of quasi-scientific complexity that the language of explanation turns into a rhetoric of obfuscation. Avidan's poetry includes much clever humor and parody, convincing messages of social and moral concern, and many personal expressions of quietude and love. The hallmarks of his work, however, remain these: a structure of random association, a persistent self-consciousness, a rhetoric of inflated diction, and an attitude of unmitigated oppositionism.

FROM *SOMETHING FOR SOMEBODY* (1964)

Longterm Hatred

Apparently
You hate most of the people
Who live with us and who live with you. They'reall
One big enemy and they're not so smart. Even
The best among them—beware. But
Essentially we're talking not about the kind of
Feeling that's mainly pettiness and conflicts of
Interest and a climate of threat. Conflicts
Always feed on society's primal stupidity,
Its primitive nervousness, narrowmindedness, hysteria wasted on
Petty desires. You're really
Devoid of that divine patience, which causes a
Snowball on a hill to turn into
X number of bathtubs full of cold water. Instead
Of being sovery careful of human, tidy tact on tiptoes
Of enforced silence, the concessions, the pragmatic diplomacy, which
Even while making love drums
Its skinny fingers with metal rings on the lace border
Of the sweaty blanket as on
A gold cigarette case on the edge of a table
At some nightclub, instead of being
Measured and mannered and sociable ad nauseam, you always
Project a warlike attitude toward things. Somehow
Sometimes it's even easier, eventhough
In the final analysis, it's a heavy, a very very heavy
Burden. Friendship
Becomes the highest peak of the human
Perfections that move inside you. War—
A tiresome history of useless shellings, which somehow
Construct the meaning of your rampant breathing
In the land of the living, pointless battles, always pointless, but
Together they constitute perhaps the loftiest of battles

Known to humankind. Personal honesty
Is the constant cause of war, and it's also
The arms and ammunition and even
The totality of losses in battle. Hypocrisy
breathes only the air of appeasement. Perhaps
In this way human culture was created. Gradually
you begin to grasp the full meaning
Of your place here among the people. The collective
projects, the inheritance of generations, the humanism,
Which is the good-hearted father of them all, most are totally empty
Of personality and character. Accusations
Are the rare climaxes of your poetry. Pain
Is a low-oxygen wind which blows on distant heights. Snow,
Except for a very few private occurrences, always
Always stays frozen and unfriendly and frigid, always
Frozen and unbefriended and almost unbreathing, but always
Always very close to the sky. The sun
Is a hot and bright and gigantic illusion, which
Has among other things a concrete existence. The exact
Sciences are always able to utter
Some wise words on the subject, but
That's not the point. The snows on the heights
Are the sun's nearly unconquered competitors, they laugh
At her from within the white death. Somehow
Sometimes they're her only friends. The sea at least
Is certainly beautiful, certainly beautiful. You perceive
A very concrete conceptual pattern, that hatred
Grows firstofall on the background of the narrowness of places and the
    laziness and limitations
Of beings lacking momentum and goodheartedness within
A very densely oxygenated atmosphere. For there
They kill the wondrous snows even with their feet, but they'll
Also never understand the sun. In the vast
Spaces of spiritual freedom, perhaps someday you'll be able to march in
    them alone, as
At the funeral of all humankind, butnot
As a sole and solitary human witness, perhaps you'll learn
To wring out of yourself a good apologetic smile and to grasp
The ancient pains of the land of enslavement from which you fled,
From the horribly infantile matter, forever whimpering
Like a hungry infant in a filthy crib or like
A blind kitten on wet sand or some
Other animal cub. Only there

In the vast spheres of freedom,
Of this flight, of this sovery
Longterm hatred, to die—
That is, to see for one continuous moment-of-dying
The beautiful land beneath you. The valleys,
Therefore, are really only a part of the whole. There's certainly
An endlessness of looks, but it's all
Beautiful and spacious and beloved, at least
When you look at it from on high, when the light
Allatonce freezes in the pupils of your eyes like a magic diamond
Of childhood dreams of dwarf fairy tales, when dying
Is the only certain situation in your brief biography, and the look
Is clear and sober and final. And then in vain
Your dead hands suddenly rise up
With some insane wish to return, to return below,
To return and to concede. Surely
The high snow and the valley
Will not surrender their old friends. Death
Patiently envelops you and rolls on
It matters not where. The sun
Surveys the high white plain
With a look of acceptance, it seems, as if
Once again it's suffered a minor defeat, a very
Minor defeat, eventhough
The victory is a major victory indeed.

Recurring Opportunity

Seeing means going far off, going off down the road,
Folding up all memories, closing all openings,
Obscuring all transparencies, seeing in them only useless excess,
A superfluousness of all kinds of coercions.
Going far off means not seeing, not seeing down the road,
Opening all forgettings, forgetting all openings,
Downplaying transparencies, seeing in them only a road
Leading to and not back from all kinds of coercions.
Going and not returning, returning a distance,
When all the forgettings are remembered and all the rememberings are
    forgotten.

And if the transparencies are obscured, it proves that even through
Untransparencies one can see only more coercions.

Prehistory

I remember myself waiting,
Armed with a club from the Stone Age,
And I remember myself beating
With precise intelligence on straw.
Intently watching the burning of
Bridges large and small,
Happily greeting the storm of
Black snakes and vipers,
Intending to do things
No one's bothered doing before,
Organizing races of dark and light
Leopards for all my friends,
Waiting for good Death
To skip overme and go somewhere else
I've forgotten most things by now
Not remembered the least.

Some Futureplans

Let me be a mummy. Wake me up
Once in a thousand years with a massive shot of adrenalin,
I'll burn down Rome again, I'll report the event
With pallid face and pounding heart, first I'll castrate
All the barbarian warriors who'd attack it, then I'll screw
Their young women, so there'll be
Something to burn down and castrate a thousand years from now.
I have patience when it comes to
Longrange objectives.

A Moment Ago

That transitory moment between
The jump and freefall is
The worst, precisely
Because you know, more than anyone
You know, just as you've already
Been careful to point out on another
Solemn occasion, that there is no,
No other force which can check
Your last, decisive jump. But
That transitory moment is even more frightening, because
You don't know, you only imagine, you don't
Imagine, you only hope, you don't hope, you only
Guess, you don't guess, you
Know, that there is,
There is a force which can check your last jump,
And that force is none other than your last jump.

Glimpse of an Open Dream

1. Psychotherapy

The seven lean cows
Said to the Nile, in the name of
The forest: Die,
Die, die, o child. It's worth
Your while. Tomorrow you'll find
Fine gold cradled in the wind
Between the terrible reed stalks.

2. Contra Therapy

The seven fat cows
Said to the forest, in the name of
The Nile: Grow,
Grow, grow, o death. You
Must. Tomorrow the pale
Fire shall rise from the bush
And come into touch with you.

3. The Sketch

The seven lean cows
Said to the seven fat cows: Enough
For now. Both the Nile and the
Forest are ready for a truce. Now let's
Finally begin arranging
The ancient affairs
Between us. Dream Number One,
Move on.

4. The Glimpser's Comment

And maybe it went likethis: The seven
Fat cows asked
The seven lean cows: How,
Really, how do you manage
To keep so trim?

From "Samson, Our Hero"

*(An interpretive lecture before the Department
of Biblical Studies)*

1. General Truths

Heroes never tire
Aslongas they don't cut their hair.
Heroes don't cut their hair
Aslongas they don't weaken.
Heroes weaken
Only
After
Meeting
With Delilah
On the
Positive
And
Negative attributes
Of every helpful female figure.

Samson was that sort of hero.
She played with the hair on his chest.

2. What Bothered Him

All gates were closed to him.
The length of his hair stood in inverse proportion
To his social possibilities.
He was a solid young man, but very much a loner.
It would be a mistake to think of him as
A virtuoso.
Nothing came easy to him.
Donkeys never turned the other cheek
To him.
Bereaved lionesses pondered him long and hard
On hot moonlit nights
He didn't like manes on anyone else.

All gates were closed to him—
So he tore up the city gate
And carried it off farbeyond
All the doorways he would never cross.
The demolished entryway awaited him
To enter it like a man,
Mounted on a donkey, head shaven,
A safedistance from the mirrorlake
Where he'd admire his long hair
And lie in wait for thirsty lions
In those truly consummate moments of inspiration.
All gates were closed to him,
Because he wasn't a very sociable young man.

3. The First Date

I think you're bashful.
You're sovery different from a Philistine.
You're just what I like.
I'll be your wife.
You'll be my wife?
I'd like to change you,
To see you change in your sleep,
To make love to you after you're dead.

6. For Advanced Seminar Students Only

I'm undecided, Samson said to the columns.
This terrible light frightens me.
A distant snow is falling on my head.
Who are you, anyway?

We're your friends, the columns whispered to him.
You've stood between us before.
Don't believe anyone but us.

I'm not the same as I was, Samsonsaid.
We too are not the same, the columns said.
It's clear:
We've been waiting for you for years.

I know, said Samson.
Butnot for this.
It's not a question of time.
By the way: What's that noise from below?
Does the crowd expect something
of me?

We've waited for you for years,
The columns pleaded.
We too want to fall—
It's our right.
You've no cause to be so selfish.

I'd forgive her, Samson said.
Butnot myself.
Are you made of reinforced concrete
Or of Amorite clay?

Forget the details, the columns urged.
The architects have long been out of the picture.
Are you ready to go?

I'm ready, Samson said.

Now we feel you,
The columns confirmed.
You're the same as you were,
More than you were.
Push and we'll turn to Philistine dust
Beneath your feet.

9. The Moral

Samson wasn't the brightest
Of men.
Too bad.
A capable young man. He had credentials
That could have been developed.

FROM *PRACTICAL POEMS* (1973)

Practical Poems

Practical poems
are poems
that practical people can read
without risking their practicality
as a direct result of their readability

However—any insult is quite unintentional—
practical poems are not poems
that put people already in the center-of-things
in the center-of-things-poetical

In Jerusalem sources quite knowledgeable
seem somewhat hospitable
but rate poetry peripheral

In Cairo, you know,
they fight on for
their poetry's honor

And we cannot refute
the love of Beirut
to appear liberal rather than docile

So in things territorial,
if not quite material,
the ecology here is all but inimical

To practical poems no one can comprehend
Certainly skeptics won't bend,
but there'll always be believers in the end

Election Speech for the Presidency of the United States of Chinamerica

Now listen I am speaking to you through the miracle of rice through steelwool through Japanese microphones
I have every reason to believe that you will vote for me in the upcoming election of your own free will
My rhetorical powers are only a part of your unbridled wisdom in the voting process
This time you will demonstrate it on my behalf alone because you have faith in me
And I, for my part, have faith in your faith and speak to you as man to man
As man to woman as dog to dog as dog to bitch I'm barking at you
Screaming at you through steelwool in the rice paddies in the gas stations
This speech that for a change I've written myself

Please take note how I thrust these wondrous lines straight at your problematic hearing organs
At your desolated hearing organs I'm throwing food that's flowing healthful fresh
Your hearing organs and my brain centers and the technique of speech and the rhythm and broken lines
I swallow your growing attention through colored straws from the corners of your eyes
I have faith in myself but doubt you and doubt my doubt of you with utmost faith
What I'm creating here seems to be a poem but it's really an election speech
You'll elect me because I've confessed my crime and because you're a party to it
This stanza was written for a change by the Chairman with a starched quill pen
At Peking airport at Kennedy at Lod you're waiting for me
You take my picture and record me and take your own picture and record me you're the media
You're a reporter a steward an exterminator a literary critic an X-ray technician a customs official
You're no dummy no one gave a damn about you and you're a munitions manufacturer
I'm your salesman a woman of valor a housewife a Women's and Men's lib organization
Put something on the stove scratch my back it's hard to talk to you on an empty stomach

I hate food and you're full of food so I'm broadcasting to you on a food frequency
Dog to dog pig to pig Chinese to Chinese Indian to Indian ulcer to ulcer
I've got something to say to you and to the others I've rejected again and again for more than twenty years
Wait for me across the street with a switchblade a sniper's rifle a registered gun
This speech that for a change I bellow at you with incredible joy

So that's it for now you understand me and if you haven't understood I piss on you
As usual I revert to the least understandable words and you'll hear from me from there, too
You'll hear about me in your underdeveloped braincenters and in your higher-than-the-apes fingertips
With your subrational fingertips you'll train a global lynch mob which will turn into your unrealized dream
From a safedistance which intercontinental missiles will not cross until and including further orders
From a point of view beyond the purview of your sight and from a point of hearing beyond your hearing mechanism
Beyond your primary nerve system and above and beyond your tissue system and the level of your vibrations
The system of debts rights emotional contracts history of culture the law of the kitchen
With fine quick steelwool I scrape the stubborn layers of fat from around your carbon-copy brain
I bleed you program you a brain open to future generations to future speeches to future presidents
And you'll vote for me even before you retire with cursing and singing
In your pitiful family albums I'm shown in a mocking slide negative
You'll leave your job your sex life your military service
You'll keep turning the pages wondering why you haven't succeeded
Why dammit you haven't succeeded in getting rid of me when you were young and strong and still active

That's the end of my speech for a change no one's
Written it down or delivered it or heard it
So the words will remain only between us till the end of the century
The White House the Yellow House the Jewish State
I gave up on all of these when I was still a child
I've made this comment for a change in all seriousness

And now if you have a minute wait a minute watch
How I take off from here speeding faster
Than the speed of sound and light and brain waves
Without any air pressure or oil pressure group pressures
And the rice cries and the oil fields and atomic reactors
And launching bases radar antennas attack stations
Above and beyond all financial forecasts
And literary political strategic criteria
And insurance companies and the institution of the family and evolution
And also watch how in every place and at all times
I'm still army and administration bookkeeping
And bakery and special interests and seeing eye and listening ear
Through steelwool through Japanese microphones through the mysteries of rice

Two Memorial Poems

1. The Tale of Father's House

He always took me to visit the squadron
He was an amateur photographer I want to fly
He took my picture in a plane in black and white
Aerial photographs in color he passed the censor
Time passed we moved she moved kibbutz
I moved an institution we moved to the city
He never forgave me

And now you're filming me for television
And asking me questions whose time has long passed

In the squadron they say that just above a cloud
He was hit and they saw him immediately
Trying to bail out
Later they found his body

And not far from it the camera
Hit by shrapnel by fire and by earth

But surprisingly still in one piece

2. The Tale of Father's House (addendum)

He took his accordion and took a shower
He wore an undershirt and did calisthenics on the grass
Fridaynite at home at one in the morning

He went back to the squadron and since then we've heard about
All the brave deeds he'd done
Years of training a real character and how
They saw him jump from the training tower
And since then the story hasn't changed very much

Minor Mythology

Between a wicked rhinoceros trail
And an astonished elephant path
A rustle soared soundlessly

And a lioness crouched over her cubs
And a primeval serpent suspended
Himself in the top of the oak
And the eagle of the sky
Made no division between the waters above and the waters below
And the wind which hovered
Over the chaosabyss
Waited with a tired flutter
For the lovely moments to come

Song of the Self-Made Orphans

We'll hoist daddy's vest
to the top of the mast
Then we'll drown him in the sea
We'll pierce his body with pine
needles and
nightingale quills
He'll fly
He'll flutter up to the sky with a sigh
A moth in cocoon a wingless blob
A stuffed songbird chirping in the dark
Thus ending a joyless career

We'll scrub the smokestack
with a hunchback
We'll toss mommy
into the sea

She'll float on the tide
in the cold of the night

She'll shake in the wind like a scarecrow

A brave new world
An open game

The water will sweep her out to sea
The sons will grieve some
They'll call her back, you see
But everything's clear cut dry it's done

The tide's an element
That escapes indictment
M-o-n-t-h-s
have passed responseless
Deaf dumb blind
and loveless

In the end a terrible wizard will put
all the children to sleep
without a peep
And even we
will swing from on high
It was fun
byebye
nighty night

Fire the Babysitter

Leaving kids alone is no problem
A child is something pretty reliable
Like a cassette
The more you press it the more it shrieks
It won't spoil it'll
Work under all conditions it's
Open to countless possibilities
There's no reason for it to stop
Working before your very eyes unless
It's deliberately tampered with.

What I Have to Tell You, Until Next Time

I love the stillness you leave behind you.
I love the death that flows from your poems.
I love the fast pace of your movies.
I love the noise that goes before you.

I love the stillness you leave behind you.
I love the grass you trample with your feet.
I love death and your lifeinsurance,
And I love your name and all you own.

I love the stillness you leave behind you.
I love the room when it's empty without you.
I love the water that flows over your body.
I love the darkness that does you in.

I love the stillness you leave behind you.
I love the rustle that trails at your feet.
I love the moment I was left without you.
I love the distant color of your eyes.

I love the stillness you leave behind you,
And I sit here thinking about you—
How big you were and frightening in your lifetime
And how I'll get along here now without you.

I'm afraid of the stillness you leave behind you,
And I sit here thinking how it will be without you,
And I remember all these things that were before you,
And I sit here in the stillness and think about you.

Burying Uncle Salomon

Wet paint on the cheeks wings and a sudden wind
No God in heaven fish in the sea birds on trees
Back on bed bed on floor colonnaded building
A flag grown cold busy people broken earth
And now two or three deep breaths and a sneeze
Messiah is born with a sneeze a donkey's bray
A swish of the tail a door slamming a shovel's clang
Messiah is born in the town's lying-in clinic

No talking twobytwo quiet in threes sixes
Wrapped in bandages stretcherbearers fore and aft
Messiah is born in a Jaffa lying-in clinic
And Uncle Salomon is buried on a hot day in Holon
Wheels aligned all in a row bumper to bumper
License plate to license plate a rise in the sand

Son of Mordecai? Son of Mordecai. And his wife and daughters
His sister her family old friends whoever knew him
The deceased never thought of the end he loved to smoke
Birds and flies nested in his hair and a poisonous snake
Lay coiled between his lungs waiting for a sign

Meet Doctor Greenstein men's internist
He often warned that the man was not taking care of himself
He'd go out on the porch to see the sun sneak a cigarette
Cough a bit groan in his pajamas ask for some cognac
Curse in Russian and he'd tell everyone to please let him be
He wants to smoke he won't stop life is too short

And now the bus halfempty halfull
Comes back to the city from the Holon cemetery
Wet paint and a sudden wind at the window
Tel Aviv's slowly growing older and Uncle Salomon's
Digging down into the earth of Holon bumming cigarettes
From all those buried there who were just as stubborn as he

FROM *MESSAGES FROM A SPY SATELLITE*
(1978)

From "Traveling in the City"

4. Three Self-Plagiarisms

Coming Home/At 5:00 A.M./& Going to Bed

A man comes home in the morning & finds himself waiting
For himself in the morning & he has nothing to wait for
& no one to wait for him in the next room in the third
Fourth fifth sixth seventh room
He waits for himself in the morning waits in the evening
He has no unforeseen expectations
He knows his place & his place knows him
& they both know themselves & each is to be respected

Not Coming/Home at 5:00 A.M./But Going/To Bed/Somewhere Else

A man yields to himself in the morning & finds himself somewhere else
He has no one to yield to & so he self-yields
Lateron he somehow leaves himself another small yield
& he's left to himself with a surfeit of yields & doesn't yield
To his legal wife to his stepdaughter to his dog
To the cat the neighbors the next generation in the line of aesthetic
    tradition
& so he's not at his desk when
Someone's needed to answer a letter someone to acknowledge
& that is really the Law in its entirety
For the masses for the Arab Peoples & for the Chosen People

Technical/Comment

Sit at your desk & slave away
Slave away at your desk hour after hour
Sit at your desk & forget there's a chair

Sit on the chair & forget your legs
Keep changing pad after pad idea
After idea & think only about productivity
That's an empty technical exercise something mechanical
Come arise o song arise o song move on

12. Another Catalogue Item

I am Walt Disney of the Kingdom of Satan
I am Ingmar Bergman of truly terrible tragedies
I am Rockefeller of unpaid securities
I am the good sheriff the bad sheriff the double-slung gunman in one
    body
I shoot the whole world & leave behind
The whole wonderful world I once could have been

18. Not Allowed to Make a Movie in This Country

Daytime. Outside. Closeup.

This country is not allowing me to make a movie
It has confiscated one of my films
It is closing off other possibilities for me

Cut to:
This is a primitive country
Which eats only what it vomits up
I'm told to write poetry speak think
But don't *show* us what you think or say
For they shall not see from afar
Nor shall they enter unto you

Cut to:
Evening. Inside. Closeup.
She won't get away with it
I have an exact list of all those who are preventing me from making a
    movie in this country
When my videocinematographic guillotine begins to fall
I'll rip them apart one by one
Perforation after perforation
Compared to me Manson will be a poodle
Hitler will be a pacifist
Ivan the Terrible will be Ivan Ivanovitch

C U T

19. End of the Trip

I'm driving a car in Tel Aviv
And what do you think happens to me at a red light
FANTASTIC
The man in the car next to me *recognized* me

He recognized me
From my one and only appearance
On the one and only television channel
In the one and only city
Where there's more or less someplace to go to
In this country.

The man recognized me and waved

DAHLIA
RAVIKOVITCH

 Dahlia Ravikovitch was born in Ramat Gan in 1936. Educated at Kibbutz Geva and at high school in Haifa, she studied at the Hebrew University of Jerusalem and later taught high school for a number of years. Her first poems appeared in the late 1950s in the famed journal *Orlogin*, edited by Avraham Shlonsky. To date Ravikovitch has written five volumes of poetry and one of prose. She has to her credit as well a number of children's books and has translated, among other works, *Mary Poppins* by P. L. Travers and poetry by Yeats, Poe, and T. S. Eliot. In recent years, especially during the siege of Beirut in the summer of 1982, Ravikovitch has become increasingly active in the Israeli peace movement. She has also become involved in teaching the writing of poetry to adults in Tel Aviv.

Ravikovitch's early poetry displays in the main romantic tendencies. The works are replete with the lure of exotic, distant places; love and lust are strong, even overwhelming; reaching beyond the normal, stretching beyond human capacities, seeking grand change—these are the recurring motifs. The poetic imagination itself seems to embody all possibilities; it is the most wondrous capability of all. The poems are also filled with mythological figures, palaces and kings, dream worlds, fairy tales, fantasies, magic, and witchcraft. The voice is often childlike, the diction archaic, mainly biblical, the rhyme singsong, the lines repetitive, as in folk ballads, for emotive intensification.

In the poem "Wind-Up Doll" (published in her first collection, *Love of the Golden Apple* [1959]), Ravikovitch created what was to become her hallmark: a voice of subtle sarcasm mocking the world's need for conformity, for expected appearance and action, for fabricated performance. In the later works, this satire of manners develops broadly into a concern for the poet's moral responsibility. The themes that predominate are empathy for the poor, the handicapped, and the downtrodden, and a quiet outrage in the face of the death and debility caused by war. The poems of a romantic sensibility evolve into a poetry of ethical sensitivity. The voice becomes more emphatic, even argumentative, unwilling to take a back seat. The speaker takes on a convincing tone and, as if lamenting the world's oppressiveness, adopts the name Ecclesiastes and quotes the opening verse of Lamentations. The strong, determined quest for sensual love turns into a platonic love of all living things, of life itself.

Accompanying the thematic shift is a change in style and structure. Although prefigured in a few earlier experiments, the change is evident primarily in the 1969 collection, *The Third Book*. Here the formally structured, often rhymed stanzas have given way to proselike lines and free-verse style. The language has lost its archaic sound; it is far more colloquial, reflecting the actual speech of everyday discourse. Among the dramatis personae in this volume are a somewhat disoriented old woman, a beautiful young boy, apparently retarded and deformed, a middle-aged war hero, his image diminished by time and normality, and the prostitutes of Hong Kong, symbols of victimization within the red-silk splendor of their surroundings. In this collection, the poet has liberated herself from the influences of her British and Hebrew poetic mentors, Coleridge, Yeats, and Lea Goldberg. The new voice, style, subject, and personae, predominant also in *Abyss Calls* (1976), coalesce most effectively into a poetry of concern and understated protest, aimed at the world's apparent indifference to hardship and suffering.

At the center of these poems is a speaker of ardent sensitivity, conveying a fervent intellectual and emotional perception that the exotic, the distant, the mythic pose possibilities only of fantasy; they are merely the simulated surface of dreams, a surface that ultimately disintegrates in the face of oppressive, degrading realities.

The figure of the poet in these poems is described as "pure crystal," a transparent mirror or clear window, one could say, reflecting "the terrible fearsomeness of our heart." Only nature—the beautiful world of birds, seasons, flowers, sky, sea—and the inner life of the imagination remain comforting forces that provide a degree of insulation against the world's sorrows. The respite, however, is only temporary: the same capacity that makes Ravikovitch a poet of nature and romance also brings her to a realization of the darker side of life. The heart is bound "with bonds of pity," for the poet, more than anyone, "knows how great human suffering is." *The Third Book* closes appropriately with "Marionette," a latter-day "Wind-Up Doll" poem, which expresses with a quiet scowl the unacceptability of indifference in the face of human subjugation.

FROM *A HARD WINTER* (1964)

Time Caught in a Net

And again I was like one of those little girls
with fingernails black from toil
and building tunnels in the sand.
Wherever I looked I saw purple strips.
And many eyes sparkled like silver beads.
Again I was like one of those little girls
who travel one night around the whole world
to China
and Madagascar
shattering dishes and cups
from a surfeit of love,
a surfeit of love,
a surfeit of love.

Requiem after Seventeen Years

The cantor would chant psalms.
The trees whispered like a gathering of black-garbed priests.
We weren't much taller than the tombstones
and we knew there'd be no resurrection in our day.
Beyond that stood the ladder raised
to the heights of the pure and holy, their souls flaming sapphires
(most of them lay in repose at our feet),
and our life was like a locust at the edge of sun and shade.
But when the drowned maiden passed through all the sea's chambers,
we knew it was the sea which gave birth to the rivers.

Tirzah and the Wide World

Take me to the distant northlands,
Take me to the Atlantic,
Put me down amid different people,
People I've never seen before,
There I'll eat wild berry cakes
And speed on a train in Scandinavia.

Take me to the Pacific Ocean,
Put me down amid the brown fish,
Amid the dolphins, sharks, and salmon,
Amid the pelicans dozing on masts,
I won't even bat an eye
When you take me to the Atlantic.

Take me to the crying rivers
And to the destitute shores,
Where kangaroo hunts kangaroo
And both are garbed in striped coats,
Bring me to the kangaroo
And set me down in the forest marsh.

Wait for me in the belly of the ship
And set me up an electric train,
I'll come quickly
To live among different peoples
I'll grin among the strangers
Like a salmon in the sea.
If you cannot give me an ocean
Give me mountains coated with snow.

Set me down among Christian sailors,
Bring me to the Norwegian coasts,
Bring me to the Australian desert
Most wretched desert in the world;
I'll teach the kangaroo
To read and write, religion and math.
Tell these strange people
I'll be with them soon.

Tell them I'll be
In the midst of the sea next year;
Tell them to ready their nets
And pull up for me
Ring after ring.

War's End

He came at midnight, his legs cut off,
But his old wounds had long since grown new skin,
He came by the third-floor window
How wondrous it was the way he came in,
We'd had a terrible time of sorrow
And many had lost their dear ones
In streets sown with scraps of paper
Pranced the orphans of the few survivors.

I was frozen as crystal when he came,
And he melted me like wax,
And he transfigured me as the fabric of night
Transfigures the feather of dawn.
His valor was transparent as vapor
Streaming from morning clouds.

FROM *THE THIRD BOOK* (1969)

Surely You Remember

After they've gone
I'm left alone with the poems.
Some poems are my own,
some are by others.
I prefer the ones written by others.
I stay quiet
and the welling up in my throat relents.
I stay on.
At times I want them all to go.
Writing poems can be nice.
You sit in the room and all the walls grow tall.
Colors turn more vivid.
A blue kerchief becomes a deep well.
You want them all to go.
You're not sure what's wrong.
You might think of two things or more.
Later it will pass and you'll be clear crystal.
Later still there's love.

Narcissus loved himself so much.
Only a fool wouldn't know he also loved the river.
You sit alone.
Slowly the faded figures vanish;
later the flaws vanish, too.
Then the sun sets at midnight.
You even remember the dark flowers.
You'd like to be dead or alive or someone else.

There may be one country that you like.
Maybe one word.
Surely you remember.
Only a fool would let the sun set at will.
It always wanders westward early, toward the islands.
Sun and moon will come to you, summer and winter.
Endless treasures.

How Hong Kong Was Destroyed

I'm in Hong Kong.
There's a bay there swarming with snakes.
There are Greeks, Chinamen, and Blacks.
Carnival crocodiles spread their
jaws by the paper lanterns.
Who told you they're carnivorous?
Hordes of people went down to the river.
You've never seen silk like this,
it's redder than poppy petals.

In Hong Kong
the sun rises in the east
and they water the flowers with scented liquids
to enhance their fragrance.
But at night the paper lanterns whip about in the wind
and if someone's murdered they say:
Was it a Black or a Chinaman?
Did he feel much pain?
Then they toss his body in the river
for all the vermin to eat.

I'm in Hong Kong,
and at night the café lights were lowered.
Outside scores of lanterns were torn apart.
And the earth was bursting and boiling
bursting and boiling
and only I knew
there was nothing in the west
and nothing in the east.
And the paper dragon yawned
but the earth kept bursting.
Hordes of enemies will come here
who've never seen silk in their lives.

But little whores still receive their guests
in stained silk gowns
in little lantern-filled cubicles.
Some of them weep in the morning
over their rancid flesh.
And if someone's killed they say:
Wa-as h-he Black or Chinese?
Poor thing, hope he didn't suffer much.

The first of their guests already come at twilight
like thorns in live flesh.

I'm in Hong Kong
and Hong Kong's on the ocean
suspended like a colored lantern on a hook
at the edge
of the world.
Maybe the dragon will
wrap her in red silk
and drop her
into the starry abyss.
Only the little whores will weep into silk
that men are still
are still
pinching their bellies.

I'm not in Hong Kong
and Hong Kong's not in the world.
Where Hong Kong used to be
there's a single pink stain
half in the sky
and half in the sea.

Sinking Rising

Now the moon is
shrinking sinking
wan and low,
lost and slow.
And even so
maybe rainclouds swell its belly,
it does seem larger.
A thin veil drifts over the sky.
The moon is shrinking sinking,
coming apart,
falling down.
These filmy clouds
have rotted it away.
But wait a moment,

behind it
a pale disc is rising,
a crescent moon
which crossed the sky before it
is on the rise.
Plain as a seed in the web of sky,
thick as a ripened pumpkin.
It's the sinking moon
it's the falling moon,
darling come look at it,
it always comes back.

Portrait

She sits home for days on end.
She reads the newspapers.
(So what, don't you?)
She doesn't do what she'd really like to do
she's got problems.
She'd like some vanilla, lots of vanilla;
give her vanilla.

In the winter she's cold, really cold
colder than most people.
She dresses warmly but still she's cold.
She'd like some vanilla.

She wasn't born yesterday, if that's what you think.
It's not the first time she's been cold.
Not the first time it's winter.
Actually, summer's not very pleasant either.
She reads newspapers more than she'd like to.

In the winter she won't budge without a heater.
Sometimes she tires of it all.
Has she ever asked much of you?
Admit it, she hasn't.
She'd like some vanilla.

If you look a bit closer, she's wearing a checkered skirt.
She loves checkered skirts because they're so gay.
You'd laugh to look at her,

It's really pretty silly.
At times even she finds it laughable.
Winter's hard for her, and summer's worse.
Go ahead, laugh,
a mimosa, you could say,
a bird that can't fly;
there are lots of things you could say.
She's always wrapping herself in something, and then she chokes,
a checkered skirt or sometimes something else.
Why, you ask, does she wrap herself up to the point of choking?
These things are complicated.

It's the cold of winter and the impossible heat of summer,
it's never quite what you want.
And by the way, don't forget: she'd like some vanilla.
Now she's crying.
Give her vanilla.

Dear Mickey

At night I always think of Mickey
and how nice he is.
Mickey smiled at me with his big blue eyes
and my heart stood still.
Darling Mickey, dearest Mickey.
He was once captain of a warship
he'd sail back and forth on a destroyer
sending waves crashing
between Crete and Spain.
Darling Mickey
for twenty years he's been growing smaller and smaller
he's nearly a midget
dear Mickey.

Twenty-five years ago
Mickey was a combat sailor
with gold stripes on his sleeves.
Mickey nearly burst with pride.
At night he'd drink himself blind
during the day he'd raise huge waves
his destroyer wheezed like a whale

his eyes grew teary with love.
Later everything changed.

For twenty-two years
he's not bought a new tie.
Mickey's not what he used to be.
The sea's never gleamed
as his eyes have gleamed
at Port Agadir.

Now Mickey's fifty and has two children.
His sons are grown but he's not very happy.
The passing years haven't been very good to him,
he's not very careful about his clothes.
Dear Mickey, what have I done to you?

When his big blue eyes fill with tears
they're more lustrous than lilies
more than bluebells
more than anything.

A Private View

Pain is something useless,
I say,
like a worm crawling on fruit
which then turns tasteless.
I know you
I see what your youth was like
and how your face has yellowed.
This is not how heroes are born.

Heroes are something else,
I think,
they're men who don't vegetate.
They fight in the air and on the sea and in Manchuria too.
Always somewhere remote and strange.
My heart goes out to them to the air and to the sea and to Manchuria too
but they'd best not set their hearts on medals.
Usually they're fuel for locomotives
as in Manchuria.
And I'm sorry to say they die like dogs.

Pain is something inhuman,
I insist,
I can't imagine any extenuating circumstance.
It's clearly ugliness itself:
someone lost in secret
goes on turning black
turning black and blighted
wifeless, childless.

Marionette

To be a marionette
In this precious grey light before dawn
To sprout up from under the new day
To dive
In lower streams
To be a marionette
A fragile pale porcelain doll
Constrained by strings

To be a marionette
And the strings which bear my life
Are strings of pure silk
A marionette
She too is real
She has memories

Four hundred years ago
There lived Doña Elvira the Duchess of Seville
With her three hundred handmaidens
Each time she cast her eyes
Upon her gossamer silk handkerchief
She saw her destiny:
To be a porcelain puppet
Or a wax doll

Doña Elvira the Duchess of Seville dreamt about late-ripening vines
Her knights always addressed her in subdued tones
Doña Elvira the Duchess etcetera passed on to her maker
And left her two sons and daughter
A dubious future

In the precious grey dawn of the twentieth century
How good it would be to be a marionette
This woman's not responsible for her actions
Says the judge
Her frail heart's grey as the dawn
Her body's constrained by strings.

FROM *ABYSS CALLS* (1976)

King over Israel

To Yitsḥak Livni*

Forever in the back seat of the car
the sky dry as a field of thorns
I could find nothing to rest my eyes on
from one end of sky to the other.

White nights
they're as bad as a wild beast
baring its fangs at a desert shrub.
But even nights turned black as chimney soot
would not look good to me.

This Dead Sea has no water for the thirsty
there's nothing for the eye to rest on in celestial spheres.
So many years in the back seat
like a field skipped over by the rain.

This field has no water for the thirsty.

The man who walked the streets of Jerusalem
with a crown of thorns to shame him,
he's the man who knew the taste of the field
which holds no hint of water for the thirsty.

The man who climbed the streets of Jerusalem
and from the outset saw his end before him,
great sorrow weighed down his heart
when he saw even the sky dry as a field of thorns.

And I who sat in the back seat
so many years in the back seat,

*Livni (1934–), Israeli journalist and broadcaster.—TRANS.

even I knew not to put my trust in
ships which seem to sail across the sea.

I Kohelet was King over Israel in Jerusalem.
How solitary she sits.

Man of Mystery

Aaron is a man of mystery
He doesn't behave like any other man
Sometimes he thinks he's God
Because his grandfather was a man of God.
He has a pleasant voice.
He has so much
He loses himself in his sunporch,
And not just because of the plants.
The sun lights up the leaves for him.
The threads of chlorophyll light up for him like phosphorus.
He says the heat lingers at night
But sometimes he lies,
More than anything he's lost in the desert
Sometimes he's as good as dead.
He's always traveling to distant places
Distance doesn't scare him,
Nothing scares him
Except sticking a needle in his vein.
I know him better than any friend.
I was with him when he died.

Who Art Thou, O Great Mountain

Afternoon light
in Jerusalem,
on the walls above Mamila Park,*

*The place names mentioned are familiar Jerusalem landmarks. Terra Sancta, an old convent, was used in the 1950s and early 1960s as one of the main Hebrew University buildings.—TRANS.

at the edge of Shlomtsiyon Street
and a cinema dark as a stable.
The sun turned dark for me at noon
in winter.
In the south wing of the King David Hotel,
in a store
I studied literature.
Later at Terra Sancta
I counted windows above the Mamila Pool;
and in my Talmud classes
and in linguistics
my eyes would open wide.
I napped at noon
and returned to Terra Sancta
to the fourth floor
my mouth gaping like a fish.

I was twenty
blinded
by the windows above Mamila
and the French Hospital
by No Man's Land.

I don't need Jerusalem to show off
since the day the sun's strength has grown weak
and thorns have multiplied.

And Gethsemane
and a bus coming up from the church
I saw them as a mirage
above Yemin Moshe.
What good is it to me
that all roads are open
and all dust is hard?

Human Qualities

Nothing human is alien to me
But not especially close either.
There's an unending cycle:
People cease to be
In a day.

The sun stood still in Gibeon
And the moon on high stood still.
And David Son of Jesse while still a boy
Slew Goliath,
But David is old and stricken in years
Soon the news will spread through the marketplace
Angels have overcome the earthbound heroes,
Take pity on the King's honor,
Tell not it in Gath.

And he in his death was like Saul at Gilboa,
Songs of Ascents he will no longer hear
I have no interest in this.
I'm willing to close my eyes and be still.
To seal my lips and be still.

Like Rachel

To die like Rachel
With the soul quivering like a bird
Seeking escape.
Beyond the tent Jacob and Joseph stood stricken,
They spoke of her with awe
All her days tossed about within her
Like a child wanting to be born.

How hard it is.
Jacob's love consumed her
Voraciously.
Now while the soul expires
She has no desire for all that.

Suddenly the baby screamed
And Jacob came to the tent
But Rachel feels nothing
Tenderness floods her face
And her head.

A great peace came over her.
Her breath of life will never again stir a feather.
They laid her down among the mountain stones

And spoke no eulogy.
To die like Rachel
That is what I want.

Poem of Explanations

There are people who know how to love.
And there are people whom it doesn't suit.
There are people who kiss in the street
And there are others who dislike it,
And not only in the street.
I think it's just one strength among others,
It may be an advantage.
Like the rose of Sharon
Which knows how to blossom
Like the lily of the valley
Which chooses its own colors.
You know,
The rose and the lily, when they blossom
They strike you blind.
I'm not saying this to embarrass them,
I know there are others, too.
In my opinion,
Hummingbirds are the most beautiful of birds
But whoever prefers can choose the nightingale.
Still I keep telling myself,
a dodo,
a three-year-old ram,
an apple that won't redden,
it's not me.

ORY
BERNSTEIN

 Ory Bernstein, born in Tel Aviv in 1936, earned a law
degree at the Hebrew University, served as an at-
torney in the Israel Defense Forces, and ultimately
joined one of Israel's largest corporations, Amcor,
which he currently serves as president. Bernstein was
part of the literary group that formed around Natan
Zach. In the 1970s he joined the younger group of writers associated
with the immensely successful literary journal *Siman Kri'a*. The author
of seven books of poetry to date, Bernstein has often contributed re-
views, translations, and other writings to various Israeli newspapers and
journals.

At the center of Bernstein's poetry is a vibrant sensitivity to everyday
life: sounds, voices, gestures, light, the wind, the face. The speaker, usu-
ally alone and contemplative, continually ponders events, landscapes, and
aspects of relationships, always trying to make sense of them. Most often
the mode is impressionistic: the perspective moves from one detail to
another, enumerating parts of the whole and finally evoking a multi-
faceted unity.

Bernstein is especially drawn to nature, and the recognition of its dis-
turbing dualistic character pervades his poems. Oxymorons abound: the
world is "beautiful and subjected," spring's flowering is "pleasant and
gloomy," pleasure "repels"; "Be fearful of joy," warns the voice. The
method is Baudelairean—and somewhat reminiscent of Bialik; the mood

skeptical, pessimistic. Nature, like the world as a whole, is full of "signs" of both vitality and foreboding. Beneath the surface beauty lie unfathomable "secrets."

The larger themes of Bernstein's poetry are travel, time, and love. Each theme in its way becomes a metaphor of transience, loneliness, fearfulness, sorrow. Travel fosters an illusion of impermanence. The speaker often appears to be an outsider, a stranger who may enjoy the freedom of adventure and the change of scene but realizes their transitory nature, the inevitability of returning to the commonplace. Foreign locales make only for an illusion of escape. In the end, as metaphors for Bernstein's general perception of experience, they reinforce an abiding sameness, a pathetic rootedness in the concrete world of time and daily routine.

In a similar vein, love in Bernstein's poetry reflects an ambiguous condition of security and overriding sadness. Like travel, the act of loving signifies newness and innocence, the possibility of escape, a haven from common pains. The lover, however, contemplates the aftermath of aloneness, the fragility of the transitory act. The love motifs reach their fullest expression in the uncharacteristically long poem "This Is a Poem of Love." The voice is quick to assert that "love" may not be the right word at all; perhaps "compromise" (or "standoff") would be better. Love is respite, security, excitement, even celebration, but it cannot banish feelings of loss and powerlessness, it cannot prevent a return to the ordinary and the unchanging.

In the remarkable cycle *An Evening with Sue* (1976), Bernstein creates a potent thematic combination of love, death, and loss. Sue, seemingly a bereaved lover—the entire cycle is fraught with ambiguity and is often apparitional, much akin to Alterman's *Happiness of the Poor* (1941)—is offered consolation by the speaker-visitor. Even so, the world remains "mute," "bereft of smell" (i.e., love); what's done is impossible to retrieve. In a tour de force of ambiguity, the speaker suddenly appears to be her dead lover, a ghostly reminder of the fixed nature of death. His advice to Sue is an ironic suggestion of reincarnation, an apparent affirmation of death's dominion and its incumbent burden of loss. These themes are reflected in the later poetry in recurring motifs of aging and in the cycle *With Death* (1982), poems written in response to the last illness and death of Bernstein's mother.

Bernstein's style consists mainly of a disjointed syntax. The flow of sentences is continually broken by short adverbial and appositional phrases, set off by disruptive commas. The abundance of pauses creates a hesitant tone, which renders the speaker more pensive, more taken with the details of description or experience. This aspect of style, generally responsible for the impressionistic mode, also creates a sense of immediacy, which inevitably involves the reader in a more deeply affective framework of expressiveness. Another major stylistic feature is Bernstein's high diction, buttressed with archaic words and word forms. With this diction and the use of traditional rhyme patterns, paradoxes, and skepticism, the poetry is often reminiscent of the British metaphysical poets. Two additional stylistic devices are noteworthy. The poet frequently uses the Hebrew passive-intensive verb forms, which evoke a feeling of duress, of violence or subjugation to uncontrollable cosmic forces. He also tends to list parts of landscapes, the body, or the face, a device that suggests intimacy and familiarity but often results in an impersonal blurring of the entire entity, in a failure to retain the living essence of things and of people.

Two images remain especially resonant in Bernstein's works. There is the central, speaking persona, seeking self-definition and searching for place, for privacy, for sense in a world inexorably baffling. And there is the sleeping woman, the calm, apparently self-sufficient lover, who somehow has succeeded in escaping the world's woes. For her, all is peaceful; but for the lonely, wakeful poet, aware of all the empty gestures and actions of flailing humanity, the night is long and disenchanting.

FROM *IN A SHORT SEASON* (1967)

In a Park, in Siena, at Twilight

Fall and the bees. Where do these evenings take me,
these lush evenings? By day, hectic movement
and thick crowds. And at night,
dark, gathered pines, the wind held
in them all night. Your beauty
was revealed to me all that
fall. And only in the morning,
swathed in humming and in gold, bees
surround you. Where have they taken us,
those days, growing shorter, so carefree, in this
strange land, in a garden growing dark,
the bees buzzing about? I sit and watch
the blooming, on a Monday, in Siena.
Fall tints the movements gold
and slows them down. A breeze
stirs, above the city, over there. And now,
by my side, your hands are gone, your
smell is gone, all of you, gone.
Your voice which surged, so startled,
in the dark. Bees dart down and drift off,
confining me in the midst of
a short season.

Nocturnal Journey

You go somewhere in your sleep
for you return weary, your hair disheveled,
and sometimes you say things

in your sleep as you pass by.
But I'm left here, by your side,
and the shutters' shadow slides over me
as I prepare for a trip. When you go,
please leave word of your destination:
come winter, winters perhaps, when
the city's refined by rain, perhaps
I'll be well prepared to
move on together with you. But
in the meantime, your face, as you stay
here with me, takes on the look of travelers
moving off in the distant windows
of a swaying train, already tainted
with some strange awareness.

Mene Mene

You must leave here. The signs say so:
chalk writing on the
wall, children running about,
harried, in the hours before dusk.
The sea raises its voice. You must
leave here. Voices, rising in the distance,
through the lovely windows, beyond
the lovely trees. It's been so
pleasant. You must leave here. There's no one
waiting. The stations are deserted. Cities
turn their back on the sea or
the road. You'll turn up
very late, in a small town, along the
mountains' fringe. Children will be playing
in a strange tongue. Trees, whose names
you don't know, will spread their shade
then withdraw it. A bell will call out. A train
perhaps. You'll spread out your things.
You'll look at doors. Once more
night will overtake you. You must
leave here. Bearing tidings doesn't suit you.

No one will teach you wisdom. You'll be
left alone morning and evening, morning and
evening. So how will you know
when it's time, and the time always
comes, sooner or later. You must leave here.

FROM *THEY'RE ALL SEPARATE ACTS* (1974)

Only from Afar

Only from afar do I see the hedge,
beyond it the twisted trees, the hills
of my vampire land, above them
the plane: molten, flickering, and forlorn.

Only from afar do I see the eyes,
your skin, your hair, the pillow all around,
the land around it, immersed in flashing lights.

Only from afar do I see traces
of distress. And as on a map, around
the familiar continents, the inhabited lands,
around love that's detailed and well known, there's
a deep blue. A deep and unmarked

blue of nameless sea.

Don't Count

You can't count
all the steps
that brought you here: some
weren't steps, were just a stirring,
were one fleeting morning, a clear evening
you've forgotten, were time, the movement only
of transparent shadows, hurrying, just
a momentary restiveness. Some
weren't steps at all, were just one minute,
you walked, so carefully around,
so as not to stumble or perhaps
so as not to disturb it, they were

a place familiar from dreams
you can't dream anymore, they were a snatch
of light set in formless
jewels of eternal gloom. And so
you can't count. And even all of this
is so unreal, look:
it's already changed without
the change being noticed, while
everything all around still seems the same.

From "Poems from Mexico"

To Malcolm Lowry

Cuernavaca

An orchard beyond the wall, dripping, and a peacock.
In the afternoon the rain came and stopped. The altitude
dizzies us: on the way here
we climbed upward into a cloud hovering
in a ridge between the mountains. The city
lies low and is all gardens. But the altitude
still dizzies us. Dense and defiant
the cloud obscures the mountain: shifting darkness,
high up. By the door a buzzard, curled up
and foreboding. But beyond the walls,
moist and alert, there's climbing
ivy. The pale fruit, comely,
breaks off and falls to the ground.
But beyond the wall, moistly humming, banefully
humming, lies the locked garden, planted in
volcanic earth, growing enormous flowers
totally without scent.

A Small War

Palm trees against the sky.
No one comes to see me
in the morning. The coast is
remote and rocky and it's impossible
to hear the water.

But I constantly envision the
surprising heave of the waves.

I waited all morning for some movement: my hand
still moved at will. My leg, too.
So in the meantime everything's just fine.

A land of dew and small darknesses:
A leaf, a stone, motionless above their shadow.
And by eight, when the water suddenly disappears,
it's already too late to go out.

I stay on, fighting a small war against
the constant curtailment of my place.
The sun moves onto a building opposite
like a stroke inching its way across a face.
And now the eye. And now the mouth. And
two more words.

Mayan Ruins

"To this day no one knows
why this woman and not another," he said.
In the dark pool there were algae and stubble.
A parrot shrieked and flew off, startled, like a flare.
Someone played a languid tune. Outside,
a lonely desolation of sun. "In a
foreign land the passions are surprising."
We won't leave here without changing something
within us, like someone, before going to bed,
straightening a piece of furniture, a picture. "The reason
isn't clear. No, it's not beauty. Ugliness
has a strength all its own." The glass casts a glint
of salt, a sparkle, onto my leg, your
leg, my hand, your hand, both our faces.
Here before a fleeing twilight, among
identical profiles of stone, a place
of dampness and ferns, of an impassive
extinction so dazzling there's no way
to know if this as well is not a dream,
a silly stubbornness, mine and yours. "At times it seems
someone's saying something through us, something
pressing, relentless. And that's love." Darkness
comes on suddenly here. No one

says anything through us. In the morning
we leave here for another site, further
on, in the forest.

Universal

When he died, far away, no one at the Café
Universal heard about it for years. An old woman,
who'd sold him tomatoes, remembered a
bearded, pale, red-eyed man.
"He drank lots of water in the morning."
On the walls of the room, which you'd glance at
nervously, because someone was there,
someone who'd always elude you, a shadow,
a vapor, a glimpse of a hand—there hangs a
landscape. They don't remember you
in Cuernavaca. Old men sit in the
Universal waiting for the promised
sun, there it is, over there, beyond
the Palace of Cortez. "Who?"
It's not important. He stayed here
only a short time. "They all come and go.
Many die here. Old people. It's cheap."

Of All the Splendor

Gradually even this disappears. What remains
of all the splendor? The look of a child,
of a shrub, a sky of blindness.

I saw these very days
drawing near. Now they've
a touch of the shadow of death.
Unblemished and brief, a memory
dissolving before sleep.

A friend came to see me this evening.
I opened a door. From his place
he came into mine.

He talked but I heard very little.
Most voices are hard to hear.

Much is sundered on evenings like this,
and falls, soundlessly, for hours on end.

FROM *AN EVENING WITH SUE* (1976)

Her Words from the Corner

"At first there were men, all sorts of men, and not one at a time,
and sometimes not just one," she said. Her voice was fluid and paused
only to recollect, as if she'd forgotten some
detail or as if they could still be conjured up, all those
scenes, all those touches, the light that came this way
or that, the words that surely were said, they're always said,
and tried to stop, to quicken or conceal. "And later—women."
But that's all over. "That's all over. So many different bodies. Only
a radiance on the retina remains, like after
staring at a light. And nothing more."
Tall trees loomed in the windows. Her face
leaned back and forth, her words from the corner,
like faceless, unending hosts. Her hands lay
in her lap, her collar fastened, her buttons
were all fastened. That same body set into her clothes,
and her hair was bound in braids. I didn't say a word.
And in the window stood the bare trees that nothing
keeps from budding again and again,
in their true time. "I'm thirsty,"
she said and got up, and on her leg was
the mark of a dark bruise, like a soft spot
in fruit, ripened at the end of a branch and waiting
to fall, untouched, unblemished, to the ground.

What She Didn't Say

And when I lie between the standing walls,
and the radio sound is with me in the dark,
playing music that always crosses space

and moves about, unseen,
I lie there waiting for a face, to see
someone's come to stay a while,
eyes dilated, to see it soon above me.
Plants are fertilized from afar, only
the animate are encumbered with contact, the onus
of coming face to face. Perhaps someday,
I could, from the periphery, just signal,
without coming near, or touching, the air
alone enveloping and joining us, distant, and later
the music hasn't changed, outside
the houses are dark already and indistinct,
a sign of light. And everything's
still in place, as if nothing's been missed
or added, but someone's been here and gone and left behind
only a strange scent that won't so quickly fade.

Memories of Her Friend Who Died

When he first came to see me I forgot that he was dead:
He wore familiar clothes and smiled a lot.
And I hadn't touched a man since he died for fear of limbs falling off
because he'd been buried with no coffin and quickly decomposed.
And when he came he sat still, preoccupied with something
unknown and provoking, just as he liked
to play with his voice, the style of his hair, with my body,
only his forehead kept twitching for no reason,
like someone looking into the distance, the sun striking his eyes.
And I went to him and told him things that he knew,
a story I'd tried to tell him before, memories,
silliness we'd seen together. And he didn't answer.
Outside rose the strong earth smells
and I knew: He'd always
return in this sort of rain and what would I tell him next time or next
    year or years,
if not the very things that today, that again, and again and again.

An Imagined Description of Myself, in Another Scene

Tanned young men about to dive,
In yellow wetsuits, replete with gear,
And sounds of bustle among the boats
Carrying them to the specified spot,
Where solemnly they'll sink into the water,
And then, silent, descend till they fade into sight,
And I sit by them, seeing them set
Around me, stern, purposeless playthings,
Seeing them move off in shallow glimmers
On a sea lit for hours and lit after them,
Seeing them wrapped in splendor,
And then, in the depths, surely
in a place I'm not equipped to reach,
By the unremitting cold of the water.

What She Wanted to Be

A morning of evanescent shadow, of laughter
of unknown source. In an elegant
trimmed garden you're with them all.
Carefully you avoid
the creeping grasses, try
not to remember your recurrent dreams
revealing unfamiliar people
gesturing obscurely in their haste,
and the signs you discover on waking
convey an imperfect meaning
which can't be explained away. And then,
as you limply close your eyes,
floating bubbles of brilliance rise before you,
bursting at their limit. A wondrous
balance to the table, the lawn and glasses
set carefully, for a while, around you,
and your hand, you lean and watch to see it tremble,
and you wait for the brief, slight motion,
frightening, since there's no more reason to depart,
and when it's over, you come back, but not quite.

And Later by Myself

Come lie down next to me and rest.
Clouds are passing soundlessly.
Rain tumbles down, mute. A city
devoid of speech. Nothing
will come here quickly, it's already
gone astray and dwindled. I won't hear
when you leave: A door will close quietly
at the photo's edge. Some
watchful trees are there, a fleeting
effulgence, a stirring
rife with ghosts. And
I don't remember too clearly, blot out
all that's been,
and light strewn in my morning that's
slowly revealed like
the bare, brawny back
of someone who won't turn around.

And after a Long While

In this place they make small gardens bloom,
create all sorts of scents, stay confined at night.
Chance is no cause for sorrow, even the passing
has become, elusively, permanent, time
that's past, that's passing.

Only at times, Sue, when evening's
on the small gardens, on
the mowed mounds of grass,
I see in fragments once again
the total construct of your face: how
eyes and mouth are set in it,
how hair's above, how the hands.

As evening falls they turn up the lights
at home. The moon's in place. A year
in its fixed cycles.
All you need, Sue,
is to be born again as an animal.

FROM *COMMON GROUND* (1979)

Time to Leave

Summer. Time to leave
the place we've grown used to,
the plunder of recurring gestures, the quest
for a spell soon to be lost. It's already
summer. Time to leave all this, time
to listen, on the seared mountaintops,
surrounded by a day that's gone well,
to the pipes of fertility, delicate, hollow,
among the sheltering reed huts.
A moment of summer before we're brought down,
before I'm returned to the places I know,
at the foot of the huge piles of tools
at the approach to the courtyard of death.

A Wind, That Comes on Suddenly

A wind, that comes on suddenly, restores
true dimension to things gone awry:
distinct details in an impartial light.
Yet, in its fleeting effort, there's
a fearsome semblance of life, as it stirs
the scarecrows suspended at the field's edge
to frighten off the birds. And we,
in the cumbersome silence, on some patio
covered with gravel, grow accustomed to the qualms
contained within. Transparently,
trivial things converge about
whatever we were then, on the patio,
herding us closer together, drawing

precise margins to whatever we do.
A conversation—we've forgotten when it began—
with someone whose face is indistinct
explains events much better than before.

At Woods' Edge

At the edge of the woods where people
who love their work
whistle among the branches
I stopped, without entering
the full thickness.

All is stage-like and ripening.
But whoever hesitates like me
won't step into the woods,
his soul beset
with bitter signs.

Whoever is fearful of hearing
what must be told
will stop, like me, on the path
which raises the hot dust
and wait for the darkness
to find his way home.

This Is a Poem of Love

This is a poem of love, outspoken,
and, as it should be, complete and flawed,
by itself, undefined, undaunted,
with a full measure of sadness.

Love is not a word for us, too fearsome to touch.
How else might we call this middle ground,
these pleasures devoid of recurrence, this thing which stems
the hurried pace? One must uphold the here and now.

Tell me, where does your sleep wander at night?
Will you go after it, leaving behind
dishes and rooms, traces of the commonplace
which appear, in the dust, by our bed?

We'll not gather, we'll not succeed in gathering
everything we should gather,
so as to store it by the sides of the dead, to sustain them
on their visionless journey. But something
is gathered. Something, a tiny amount, accumulates.
We'll have to take risks, to go forth with these provisions,
to approach with these hands. We've nothing more to offer.
Anything else has been beyond us.
Stay here a while longer. Watch over the spoils
with me. Everything's still all right.
Luckily, not everything's yet in place.

I've seen women risk their bodies
to kindle compassion, tremble
from passion's routine, one
after the other, leave puddles of love around them,
growing smaller and smaller. Then they go and move on,
carrying with them in their vaginas
small portions of seed, life
stored away not for them.

Days pass and turn shapeless, there's
nothing that does not disappear.
And meanwhile I see the strong lights
through you,
as through a curtain that won't close, on a night
of troubled sleep, see you gather them up,
hold onto them unknowing,
thinking that you're all darkness.

You darken the doors with transparent paper,
and in the mornings you scrub stains of saliva from the windowsills,
you notice that time is unchanged
by the growth of shrubs in the yard, by the sudden cracking
of china in the cabinet. And only in the evening
when weariness quietly splits
the delicate mask of death
which the soft light of the side lamps
has fixed on your face, as if to prepare
your body for its dust, you come back, suddenly
from your solitude to the unclean, to the deranged, to change,

to remorseless deed, to the festivity
of shadows, of a passing shadow, of the grass of the fields.

You've never spoken a word of love to me.
Faithfulness is your failing. But between us
there are ways of travelers who help each other.
Surely we've traveled far, and anyway
there's no one near us.
So say it quickly, now, before it's evening,
when everything trembles with color
thrust into it just before dark.
Along your periphery there's a reluctance, a hint of transparence,
a thin film concealing you. Hold only onto the obvious.
And leave signs. Only young men
count their lovings,
but we, dark wonders, will survive
at the fringe of a building rising along with us.

Your actions are already unerring.
The humane, which protected us,
has already lost its power.
You're already another, and like others, flawless.
Closeness already blurs your face
like an oversized enlargement.
No longer familiar, we'll still have
a time of mutual help before departure.
Perhaps there'll be a cycle of violence,
in unfamiliar quarters, where we may find ourselves.
Ferocity will make us realize the main thing,
forgotten out of grand, ungenuine bliss.

When I'm here, you go on there with what you're doing,
repeat, with measured movements, things that already occurred.
Fearing collapse, you don't change a thing.
You go out only at times, under an eclipse,
to wait for someone who won't be me,
who won't be coming, for he's never yet come.

Games

Pass over this as well,
move on: far from sight,

far from the heart, especially when the heart
again is no precious tool, extinct
in times of trial, again nothing more
than a heart grown in the tangle of veins,
like a head thrust into the thicket to look.
So pass over this as well, move on,
because of a sin I committed in a moment of weakness,
I stopped, by chance, within range of the trivial,
far from sight, far from the heart,
watching how children hide,
at the close of an unremarkable day,
close to each other even in hiding,
their game innocent, striking terror.

A Season when Nothing's in Place

A season when nothing's in place
comes on like a dream, conjuring up
unadorned buildings, suddenly,
in familiar neighborhoods.

Objects grow distant from us, speeding, as
from an odious center, into unsurprising space.
And it expands around us, and we have more room.

And like feathers from an invisible nest above,
fragments, flowered and opaque, flutter down,
traces of a graveless death.

All This Is My Time

All this is my time. No time to seek disguise. There'll be
no sign years later of a different shade
at the spot where we stood, like the mark left
when the furniture's moved.

And as in disturbed waters
we can't bring ourselves to completion.

Only at times do we take on rigidity,
when we move, a time of transition,
a momentary image, mostly doubt, a shape
dispersed in a flash.

To us it seems, after the fact,
that others have seen us, fragmented,
as we are, as we'll yet be,
as we'll be retold, if we're ever retold.

More Questions

When we returned they asked us questions,
the answers to which were far more alarming.
We could have said we were at a forest estate,
a stone castle, a garden, and at night
horses stamped their hooves in the stable.
That would have been enough, and,
in fact, we don't have to answer
to anyone, but standing face to face
what bothered us was the deceit
which began long before now,
a flaw pervading every image.
The listless incline of the hills
revealed a tree or a house, remnants
afloat upon mighty waters. This we saw. That's right.
Perhaps you'd see it differently.
You'd see a matchless valley, a purity unblemished,
a light obscuring all transience.

MEIR
WIESELTIER

Since the beginning of his writing career in the early
1960s, Meir Wieseltier has aligned himself uncom-
promisingly with a modernist, nonconformist literary
stance. His poetry resounds with sardonic declara-
tions on love, society, and life; it reflects a fervent dis-
dain for bourgeois mores, religion, and politics; it
openly proclaims the poet's antipathy to sentimentality and all other ro-
mantic notions. Wieseltier's poems focus on themes of loneliness, frustra-
tion, and the premature loss of youth and innocence; they bespeak a
pervasive bitterness and a wished-for but unredemptive death. His poetic
voice urges philosophical and emotional involvement, a full awareness of
the shallowness of ideologies, of the unnerving terror of war, of people's
brutality toward one another, of life's utter emptiness. The tone is sar-
castic, mournful, obdurate; the rhetoric is by turns quietly despairing and
bombastically demanding. The imagery is often ironic: it combines ro-
mantic possibilities with unmitigated realities; it depicts love, beauty, sen-
suousness, only to destroy them with obscenities or fiery visions of doom.

In this poetry of iconoclasm and protest, Wieseltier generally demon-
strates the influence of French surrealism, especially Apollinaire's free-
verse style, forceful irony, and heightened imagery. Wieseltier has also
been drawn to Anglo-American poetry: there are allusions to and bor-
rowings from Yeats, Eliot, and cummings. Mayakovsky and the rhetorical
bombast, cynicism, and experimentalism of Russian futurism have also

influenced his work. In the tradition of contemporary Israeli poetry, Wieseltier is clearly heir to Natan Zach and David Avidan. The inheritance is structural and linguistic as well as thematic. Zach's playful and emotive repetitions of words and phrases, his use of balladic dialogue; Avidan's endless anaphoric lines, declamatory rhetoric, neologisms, and morphological elisions and disjunctions—these are some of the stylistic devices adopted by Wieseltier in the bulk of his poetic works.

At the center of most of his poems stands Wieseltier himself, an engaged, moralistic presence, pitted against innumerable situations of social and intellectual stress, continually projecting a stance. For Wieseltier, "art for art's sake" is clearly an ignominious doctrine. He goes beyond Zach's ironic understatement, that poetry is "something that leaves something behind," and proclaims it to be a kind of nothing: "Take poems, but don't read them. . . . spit on [this book], crush it, / twist it, kick it / throw this book into the sea." Poetry and its readers are held up to ridicule; one is useless, the other effete. Poetry evinces only a "lust for lies" and "word tricks," and Wieseltier appears to regard it with disdain.

The antagonistic posture, however, seems to be only a cover for the poet's self-identification. He is a lonely voice, even a prophetic voice, which goes unheeded in "this world of dust and consuming fire." As a poet-philosopher-moralist, Wieseltier has embarked on a search for values in a chaotic, unredeemable universe. The poems embody his identity as a guardian against the forces of the philistine world. He writes as "one who has the strength to take a stand"; the alternative is to accept a fate of surrender and mediocrity. Trapped in an instinctual but futile activity, he is committed continually to speaking out.

Wieseltier, on the one hand, perceives the poet as damned by the "judgment" of words, oppressed by the relentlessness of poetic thought. On the other hand, poetry is revitalizing: it allows one to draw "another circle on new sand," to erase and start over. The poet is an outcast, the dross of society, an unfulfilled, frustrated observer of human faults; but his very rejection denotes his moral superiority, the victory, however Pyrrhic, of an intelligent, sensitive awareness over society's sham and self-inflicted sorrows. Poetry offers the opportunity to observe life, to describe its sweetness as well as its bitterness—and Wieseltier often presents poignant, lyrical portraits of emotion, people, and landscapes. The overwhelming feeling, however, is that he is at odds with the unsavory, unmitigated circumstances of contemporary life.

Wieseltier was born in Moscow in 1941 and arrived in Israel in 1949. Raised in Netanya and Tel Aviv, he studied English literature, philosophy, and history at the Hebrew University. In the 1960s he spent some time in England and France; for several months in 1982 he held an International Writers Fellowship at the University of Iowa and traveled extensively in the United States. Over the years Wieseltier has been active in several literary journals. With the help of a group of young poets—among them Yair Hurwitz, Aharon Shabtai, and Yona Wollach—he founded in the sixties the "little magazines" *Peshita* and *Gog*, which adopted an oppositionist stance toward the poetry of the 1950s. Through the seventies he was active in *Siman Kri'a*, coediting several issues. An adept translator—translation is his livelihood—Wieseltier has published a collection of verse translations, mostly from British poetry, and a translation of Virginia Woolf's *To the Lighthouse*. In early 1984 he was awarded the prestigious Elite Jubilee literary prize.

FROM *CHAPTER A CHAPTER B* (1967)

Take a Look at My Rebels
Verses on a motif of Jerusalem and feet fire and wood

Take a look at my rebels
my skinny-legged rebels,
Yohanan of Gush-halav was lean and beloved
and Shimon of the Desert*
had flat feet.
(not one cross but three stood
                    on Golgotha.
and in Galilee no one cried much for twice the number).
the one who did the nailing was an expert
and the one who made the crosses did an honest job.
laborers enlisted for Roman workshops
                    slaved
in the streets of Jerusalem.

where housing projects now stand, crosses dreamt
of newcomers.
and the rain fell like a lattice, and the blood
mixed with dust and wood.
and hearts mixed with vengeance were
red and subdued,
and my rebels drank cheap wine and said:
wait, we'll be drinking *lechayim* in Pilate's cellar.
and when they pulled up their robes
they were skinny and consumptive
and had flat feet.
and Yohanan of Gush-halav was lean and beloved
and didn't know Bar Giora by sight,
(and in Galilee no one was upset to see
the sign of a cross against the sky).

* Yohanan of Gush-halav and Shimon of the Desert (or Shimon Bar Giora) were leaders of
the Jewish rebellion against Roman rule, 66–70 C.E.—TRANS.

Josephus told you none of this
                          though he knew
they'd not be drinking *lechayim* in Pilate's cellar,
(Pilate was dead)
and his heart was as cold
as a Roman legion
facing the alleys of Jerusalem.

and my rebels wore clothes
which made them look
like wind-torn trees.
and they knew that in the end
only on a bed of flame
they'd find some rest.

and Bar Giora lingered in the wilderness
and in Jerusalem people sought peace and security
and in Gush-halav men played
with iron
and made ready for the test.

and the rain stammered on the roofs
                          and whistled
melodies.
and lizard-like heavy-hooded sleepy-eyed
legions took positions in the mud.
and at dawn with blue lead
crosses were traced against the sky.

and when a new governor took office, he shook
hands with each centurion
and the elders of Jerusalem.
and the city shook as on a swing.
and my rebels stared,
and drank cheap wine and said:

but sometimes speech froze on their lips.
and they pressed against the window and heard the noisy hammers
of honest workingmen.

Song of the Last Soldier

A song of the last soldier
in a regiment undefeated, till one day

it learned that it was quite unneeded.
And a flag as good as orphaned
was laid among the blackened forest trees,
and whoever wouldn't shoot himself
clung to their blackness until he disappeared,
and the winds blew through his ribs
or settled in his skull to take a rest.

But I hid away
the brass insignia turning black
almost like forest trees.
That very day
I ate roots and toadstools,
I slept on a branch
without dreaming.

Yesterday, the day before
the skies preached no peace,
the skies preached nothing,
and everything was allowed,
the rain that fell was brave.
I saw my brave brothers
turn to wood,
I saw the winds laugh
and the whoring earth bring forth buds.

I'm going back.
This morning I'll be passing
through familiar country, paths trodden smooth
by frantic marches.
And I won't say too bad for the toadstools
they've spoiled. I'll sit down
at noon to eat. When I'm through
I won't bury the leavings underground.
Later a red sun
will light my way reminding me unmistakably
it's the familiar I follow,
should I turn back,
I won't be led again to the main path,
the one which parts from the forest
and conceals a past that's so like tomorrow.

I saw the winds laugh
and the whoring earth bring forth buds.
I'm going back.

This morning I'll be passing
through familiar country.

Saul Re-enthroned

Fresh oil pours through your curls,
do you feel the subtle difference, Saul?
What's one oil from another, the look on the spectators' faces
is not much like spring anymore, the time that's elapsed
between enthronements
like a blackout forcing a pause in the music
has salted hearts,
has seasoned derision,
has sullied innocence.
The "Who needs it!" is already being said
(in whispers at first)
The "Each man to his tent!" bubbles up,
waiting wearies
the mind,
hearts flower but fleetingly
such is the nature of things, things
novel yet unhoped for
already course through your veins, you're given
a new sword, soon to play a role,
a gift
from the military which betokens its
confidence anew on this solemn occasion, Saul.

FROM *ONE HUNDRED POEMS* (1969)

Allenby

Suddenly leaves struck the street
And a stifled shiver rose
To become an elegy on love's
Severed tongue.
And the brilliantined flowers
Turned their heads from the wind
Which shoved them against windows
Where mannequins stood
In pressed suits
Like idols blind
Deaf, mute, in a
Ravaged city.

Poetry's Buried

At times each poet imagines himself
The last poet on earth.
Why should it be any different?
The world is dust and consuming fire.
Every grocery's a volcano.
The world, streams of turbid water and eroding
Bursting rock
Poetry?
Poetry's buried. A bastard daughter
To man's designs in nature,
To lust for copulation and rapine.
Chance cast several glances at it,
Chance is gone. Poetry's buried.

There's the sound of a poem, will it sound on,
But no one hears, no one will.
Too much noise
Something more important stronger more enduring
Consumes it. Poetry's buried.
(Like a nameless island
In the ocean wrongly called Pacific:
Some captain or other reported
Sighting it. A geological mission
Discovered it waterlogged. Someone
Who took it far too seriously and went forth
Hoping to find it
Was wrecked on a reef.)

Here in Netanya

Autobiographical Excerpt, 1950–55

We plotted our future, the young city
Was old enough for us.
We figured it out: When we were born she was seventeen.
She could have been our mother.

Some of us were biblical, some were Karl May-niks*
On the Sabbath we'd wander the dunes northward
Over the sea cliffs
A dream ladder cawed to the top of the water tower.
Courageous we climbed, courageous
On the coil of scorching concrete
We glanced sidelong at the sea
We screamed into the Sabbath silence

Screams like leaflets from planes
Screams upon the dessicated thorns
Screams upon the dozing neighborhoods
Steaming, know nothing about life.

---

*Karl Friedrich May (1842–1912) was a popular German author of travel and adventure serials for young people, mostly about Arab desert tribes and cowboys and Indians.— TRANS.

God's Fire upon Children

God's fire upon cities
God's fire upon homes, God's fire upon fields
God's fire is beautiful; it's kind of divine.
Flames, mighty flames, the sound of the shofar and eyes of angels.
The eyes of angels are far purer than the eyes of children;
Seraphim hallelujahs.
Children are no angels, children are filthy, children are wicked.
Children scream and scheme, bad children; rarely do they sing.
Children are no angels, their sound is no hallelujah.

Let angels come and kick the children, chase away their dirty, ugly
    mothers.
Foolish fathers, they've nothing in them of God's wisdom.
Fool fathers sow seeds of evil, harvest death, fathers cadavers.
Fathers are dirt, fathers are filth, fathers are stones.
Child, where's daddy, daddy's not up in the clouds.
Who flies up in the clouds? Not daddy, foolish, evil, daddy cadaver.
Come children, pray to God the fire, to angels lovely seraphim.
Say thank you, filthy child, miserable snotrag child.
The clouds will bring rain, nice rain all over the earth.
Angels will roll up their robes of purity, they'll give the world first aid.
And you, too, filthy child, there's a lovely cookie.
Flowers will bloom, daddy cadaver won't see the beauty.
Ugly mummy won't even look, mummy'll just keep swearing.
Angels will sing hallelujah praise God; shofars will say Oh my God.

FROM *TAKE* (1973)

Take poems, but don't read them.
Do violence to this book:
spit on it, crush it,
twist it, kick it.

Throw this book into the sea—
see if it can swim.
Put it on a burning stove—
see if it can stand the flame.
Nail it, saw it—
see if it resists.

This book is a paper rag,
letters swarming like flies, and you
a rag of flesh, eating dust and gushing blood,
staring at it half asleep.

Too Short

———begin and end inhaling exhaling
each day of our lives a slice of light and sound.

Whoever's alive after-noon
knows the morning as a story,
evening, moonlit night as a rumor,
whoever walks at night has heard about the morning,
whoever wakes in the morning is full of stories,
after-noon light and an other heat———

We'll get nothing done,
a breath so short
it's heart-rending,
whatever we'll tell our sons is so pathetic,
so slender is the thread on which past and future slide———

even so, our minds brimming, we try to lift
each day of our lives, past and future,

we try to cry out beyond the hill
to see beyond the wall———
for we've no other choice
and here's our honor, and here
we stand
in the dreadful wheeze of life's glory.

On Guard

It was a distant winter. On the edge of the flatlands
military encampments encircled dark groves,
and new fruit sucked our wasting youth
in the stupid enclosure of the supply post.

"Guard,
your song robs me of joy
and doubles my discontent.

The news you bring, I don't want to hear it
at the break of day.

Keep your news,
I tell you.

Here's a cigarette or a comb,
leave me alone with my good friend."

At night a desolation, dark and enlisted,
walked us around the warehouses.
Trickling lights fell on our stricken bodies
as we made our way from light to light.

Note

I'm buried beneath the layered debris
of my biography. There I breathe
a sure, measured breath. There I offer
gifts to all who come. There I sing
in a strong, warm voice. There
I'm plain as bread.

But my intricate biography
wraps me in shrouds of thorn,
while clods of earth and gravel
wall me off from the world of people
and their painful simplicity.

And people come, amateur archeologists,
to stick a shovel in me and gather some sherds;
and it never occurs to them
that beneath the debris I'm still quite alive,
that the sherds are only sherds
telling nothing but a few weary
episodes from my biography.

Leningrad: Picture Postcard

Leningrad brimming with rivers and canals
and squares and palaces and monuments:
a stylized history, you might say
in a grey-violet light like a stamp;

And really, like Florence, like Paris,
just a movable cardboard scene
for human misery,
brief, unmistakable, desperate,
drawn in all the rainbow colors,
but mostly in blood.

Caution Prevents Accidents

Cautiously the sun rose over the wet sand.
Cautiously the leaves began shaking off the night dew.
Cautiously the fellow draped his pajamas over the chair.
Cautiously the first buses sprang toward the exit.
Cautiously the paperboy tossed the rolled-up newspaper.
Cautiously the children chattered on their way to school.
Cautiously the bank's heavy doors swung open.
Cautiously a hundred thousand clerks sipped their first glass of tea.

Cautiously the Prime Minister consulted with the Minister of Defense.
Cautiously the postman inserted envelope after envelope.
Cautiously the harbor cranes swung their heads over the ship.
Cautiously the housewife chose the best-looking fruit.
Cautiously the Minister of Defense briefed the Chief of the Airforce.
Cautiously the students unhooked their bicycles from the rack.
Cautiously the grocer maneuvered between the fruit and the bee.
Cautiously the man crouched under the café awning.
Cautiously the lifeguard counted the heads in the water.
Cautiously the neighbor set up the folding table on her balcony.
Cautiously the Chief of the Airforce telephoned the Base Commander.
Cautiously the line grew long in front of the box office.
Cautiously the couple chose their furniture from the window display.
Cautiously the street lights blinked on one after another.
Cautiously the woman gathered the laundry from the line.
Cautiously the trembling boy touched his classmate's breasts.
Cautiously the city lights played over the dark strip of water.

    That very night a few shots were fired across the border,
    and the morning papers responded in a few lines.
    No one was hurt.
    We've not known such a strange calm for quite some time.

FROM *SOMETHING OPTIMISTIC, THE MAKING OF POEMS* (1976)

Site

At dusk they'd ask
would the sun rise again;
they ask with dreadful wisdom.
We lack this wisdom
of the powerless.

They'd be surprised at sunrise;
surprise is power.
They used this power
to dig deep pits, they
pounded rock on rock, an eternal
fire burned.

They sipped water, quenched their thirst.
They sharpened a wooden staff.
They breathed in the heady body smell,
they felt at ease.

These people, simple skulls in the dust,
could have pitied us.

❧

Everyone passes under the moon,
everyone bathes in a stretch of water,
everyone moving is watched by
a human eye, whether his own or someone
else's (even a sneak
sneaks into a lighted arena.
And as for shutting one's eyes, that blinding defense—
as for that, it's like a stick
tripping up one's feet:

Everyone passes under the moon,
everyone bathes in a stretch of water,
everyone rouses
the ripple of motion with motion.

Holy Is the Desire to Proclaim the Existence of God

In distress, in the dark.
A wounded desire, a bleeding desire,
climbs the walls.

He who sat and moaned, he who sat and kept silent.

Don't turn up your nose, don't shrug your shoulders.
Remember the golden dream, remember the shattered golden dream

Of a sudden smile, of a human glow in the eye.
Remember the choking in the throat,
the eyes going blind.

From "Elegies By the Senses"

1

Again the greyish khaki light descends
in a dense, unclean cloud
toward the gaping balconies
of our houses leaning in the sand,

Toward the facial nerves yearning
for ease with the touch of autumn wind,
a slight tremor on a scorched cheek,
again the greyish khaki light descends:

Again the greyish khaki light descends
toward shattered thoughts
on a long elliptic shape
we tried to draw again in the sand,

And on the simple meals
we set on a table in the shade of a tree
and joined together to eat in joy
again the greyish khaki light descends:

Again the greyish khaki light descends
on the wine we poured into glasses
and we leaned toward its live purple
and toward the memory of its taste last year,

And on the breasts of girls like plums
gathered into soft, undone wrappings
absorbing the touch of a hungry wind,
again the greyish khaki light descends:

Again the greyish khaki light descends
on our stricken love,
on our dissolving memories
which we planned to set apart in time,

On our flesh suddenly conspiring to crumple,
on our power to preserve the shape of a person
who might be a seeing, absorbing being,

Again the greyish khaki light descends:

Columns

1

He climbed to the treetop
Saw as far as the grove

Came down hopped
on one foot
found
palm fronds
took out his pocketknife
carved
a long sword
fenced with the air
galloped in the light

fell in the sand
got up
walked off
picked up orange
split it open
sucked it dry
threw it away
walked off

2

Yeats granted old men
madness
as their right

to be the burnt-out brain
facing the flame that hadn't touched it

to walk among
fragments of bone
still on your feet
a joke
the cheek
the lips
the palm

a joke
a black ash-strewn field flecked with grey

a joke
the burden of love and breathing
dumped at the edge of the trash heap
a joke

the city reduced to houses
reduced to walls
reduced to layers
reduced

FROM *EXIT TO THE SEA* (1981)

Love Poem

Greyish yellow is the color of the dust
that falls on cities; on a clear day
it reflects a white brilliance; on hazy days
an opaque grey. The nostrils' sensibility
seeks refuge behind the closed windowpanes
shaded by shutters.   Lines of sweltering
cars move upon the melting roads. Limbs
struck with responsibility grasp the wrapped steering wheels.
At the hour the flies slumber
air conditioners hum into the cavity of relentless space.
The grass that's left lies scorched in the yards.
The earth's furnace bakes burnt loaves of life.

Brown hair, expansive,
dances round your lovely head
that's full of skull,
eyes, teeth,
lips, earlobes,

The listening flower,
the seeing peach,
the blinking apple,
the smelling nut,
the humming pomegranate,
the thinking pear,
the crying orange,
the biting avocado,
your floating head that's washed
with tame, full-bubbling foam.

I contemplate the word *affliction*,
a word emerged from a frightful book full of fathers.
A word emerged from the mine of my mind, full of laborers,
rough men in stiff overalls and hard hats.

Showing a day's growth and grasping drills.
All my life I'll carve out just one smile.

I contemplate the word *affliction*,
a word laden with love and covered with willow shrubs.
Laden with skeletons of beasts sunk into sand, like rocks.
Like flutes unwittingly wailing a broken melody.
A word that melts toward evening as the lights come on.
Wanderlust in my bones, my palate is bitter and homesick.

A rumpled white
sheet touches
your sleeping breast.
Your nipple
rises unaware,
the sheet keeps touching.

Extended Sonnet on the Death of Isaac Danziger*

Your death in your own car
Crushed by a truck across from the hills
That tumble down like the shrill bleating
Of ewes in summer heat,
As the molten land, torn-scorched and
Dessicating secrets, shoots dum-dum
Dust at your corpse
And shuts its stony pupilless eyes,
A Nimrod, while the sun,
Oozing blood, bathes in the azure
Sea, forced from the skies
At evening, as the cry
Of women mourning the Tammuz in a rite
You'd often envisioned in the closing light
In the center of a sacred grove, while
The sun set, the sun rose on the land of silenced
Secrets you worshipped by erecting a look
To transport water, stone, wood, sky.

*Isaac Danziger (1916–77): German-born Israeli sculptor, known for his environmentally designed sculptures and monuments, including *Nimrod*, 1939.—TRANS.

From "Wintry Dawn"

12

The blood flows from my brow
in heavy, pulsing drops back
to the heart pump.
Alive, tonight
at the tattered hour of dawn
I do not count and I do not weigh.
The pool of memory, the bubbling reservoir
slowly evaporates.
With an unfamiliar gesture I forego
priority, choice,
the demand for truth.

YONA
WOLLACH

Yona Wollach, born in Tel Aviv in 1946, was raised in Kiryat Ono (of which her father, Michael Wollach, was a founder), once a rural settlement on the outskirts of Tel Aviv and now a suburb within the metropolitan area. After living in Tel Aviv for some time, she returned to Kiryat Ono to reside in the original family home. In the early sixties Wollach became part of a group of poets that formed around Meir Wieseltier seeking new directions in the formulation of Israeli poetry. She participated in the magazines *Peshita* and *Gog* and later, in the seventies, regularly published her works in the new major journals *Siman Kri'a* and *Proza*. In the early 1980s she began writing for and appearing with an Israeli rock group, Batsir Tov (Good Harvest), and in 1982 a record appeared with her poetry set to music.

The complexities of Yona Wollach's poetry are enormous. Her early work, especially *Things* (1966), often contains dramatic scenes that appear realistic yet dreamlike. The central personae have strange, Victorian-sounding names—Cecilia, Sebastian, Antonia; they appear to be facing stress, discomfort, even attack. The atmosphere is one of gothic terror; immediacy and emotional intensity prevail. Among the poet's aims seems to be a concretization of her world of rich imagination, a legitimization of random fantasies as the proper stuff of her poetry. Feelings of vulnerability, threat, and loss pervade much of Wollach's later work as well.

The complexities intensify in *Two Gardens* (1969) and in the poems of the seventies and early eighties. Generally the style assumes the character of stream of consciousness; words, phrases, and elliptical sentences are thrust together without formal punctuation, grammar, or syntax. Abruptly disjointed sequences and unexpected run-on lines reinforce the sense of confusion and incoherence. The reader confronts an unmitigatedly intense but abstract situation made all the more ambiguous by an apparently unconstrained flow of thoughts. Interpretation becomes most difficult when Wollach combines stream of consciousness with distanced, dreamlike situations (such as in the poem "At Sea"). Complex though it may be, the style clearly embodies the poet's attempt to capture thoughts and feelings and to transmit them as immediately and pristinely as possible. The reader, one might say, becomes a constant witness to the inner workings of the creative activity itself, to the poet's own active experience of expressivity.

Wollach's poetry is essentially a poetry of inwardness. It explores the inner processes of emotion and perception; it reveals the inner life of self as person and as poet. The very act of feeling is a recurrent theme. The speaker is constantly aware of emotions, their points of origin, their development, the impossibility of controlling their occurrence. The frustrations are often crushing: the continual and open sharing of emotions engenders a profound vulnerability, a nakedness in the face of probable indifference. ("I feel empty," declares the betrayed speaker.) And the most destructive force of all is the very expression of feeling itself. Once concretized, whether in words or in experience, the emotion itself is lost. "When desire has a response, it's nullified," the voice states; "feeling contains its own destruction." The externalization of feeling is less cathartic than ironic: it demonstrates on the one hand the poet's preoccupation with the emotional process and, on the other, the difficulty of capturing the emotional experience. Despite the difficulty, the endeavor satisfies Wollach's artistic insistence on giving voice to the world of the individual psyche.

Within the broad spectrum of the life of feelings, the poetry focuses on sexuality and love. These feelings are depicted as most awkward, confusing, and embarrassing during adolescence. "It's not very refined," is the teen-aged plaint. In the poems dealing with more mature experience, the tone turns more serious, angrier: cultural attitudes instill self-hate in women; it's at their expense that men continuously seek sexual variety and innovation; passion, as intense emotion, brings an unwanted, irrepressible fragility. Love can be tender, mystical, totally enveloping, "gentle as moon on water"; when its spell is broken and lovers part, it can become a "total cruelty." Love is real only in a mythic "external garden," not in the "garden of flesh and blood." Heartbreak is the repeated result; soon love becomes part of a legendary past: "once there were lovers on

the face of the earth, youth and in the end bad." Not even a princess—
Wollach's mock-heroic persona of command and control—can order the
myth back into existence.

Despite the lightheartedness and humor in some of her later poems,
Wollach's works reflect an overriding tone of melancholy, exasperation,
and bitterness. Most poignant are the poems describing her experience as
a patient in a psychiatric ward. Underscoring themes already expressed in
her poetry, the speaker-patient-observer evokes the shock of it all, the
terror, the abandonment, the abuse. The world is characterized by com-
plete powerlessness; the poems give the impression of affirming in ex-
tremis the poet's disdainful view of the outside world.

Though meager, hope is not utterly absent: it inheres in the role of the
poet and in the image of the child. As a poetic image, children, by virtue
of their innocence, are the preservers of openness and the unexpected.
While they, like adults, are victims of demons and threatening situations,
children can experience a daily rebirth that brings happiness and newness
to life. Seemingly sensitive to this possibility, the poet "kidnaps" young
people and "rescues" them in order to sustain their innocence. In this
way, poetry wins itself a continual sense of rebirth and vitality. "I'm grow-
ing a second ego like an infant in the cradle," says the poetic voice. "Con-
sciousness is our children," the voice adds, delineating the power of po-
etry to create the possibilities of true openness, to reveal inner feelings, to
affirm the great variety of individual dimensions, perceptions, and at-
tributes. Although she speaks out of a "dark, entangled labyrinth like my
soul," the poet is intent above all on the search for self, for her own voice,
for the dynamic essence of life; for "without me my life is impossible."

FROM *THINGS* (1966)

Jonathan

I'm running on the bridge
and the children are after me
Jonathan
Jonathan they shout
A little blood
Just a little blood to serve with the honey
I agree to a pinprick
But the children want
And they're children
And I'm Jonathan
They cut off my head with a gladiola
stem and gather up my head
with two gladiola stems and wrap
my head in rustling paper
Jonathan
Jonathan they say
We're really sorry
We didn't think you were like that.

Christina

They do little interminable things
They examine their big toes
The eczema on their feet
Do blacks also get eczema between their toes
They hold hands and join in
A little dance around Christina
Oh why oh why
They cry around her

Christina waits
What's your name Christina
Christina thinks and tries to feel
The circle closes in
The longing wears her down
To the depths there are many games ames ames
They lust before her and make faces at her
Her head spins amid the sobbing
And in tones of love they all
Whisper to her so what.

Sebastian

On Sebastian
Who's never existed
Not even an image
This Sebastian
A gentle feverish illness
And taking pity
I wanted to construct something in his name
Something that would embody Sebastian
Something like
An Archers' Home
Where from the casements one could see a pink city
But think of the beginning
When everything's painted and the cement's licked smooth
And the prospectus
Today I came back from another city
Where I'd always run into Sebastian
But it didn't happen to me today
I know more about it
Than what I feel
I also know that my wonderful porcelain cup
Is broken and I didn't pick up the pieces
If ever I went mad I'd build
A thousand spindles on each one
I'd put a splinter of that porcelain
Meanwhile I dream
About lakes and exotic beasts

And about the mustang lead whose presence
Again invites Sebastian.

Absalom

I must once again
Remember my son Absalom
Whose hair was entangled with my pity
But I couldn't
Put an end to Absalom my son
I'm constructing the possibilities of my feeling
Pity overwhelms me
And possibly hunger
Atavistic desires
And Absalom who wasn't allowed
In another reincarnation Absalom will be
My lover and I'll feel its memory
When Absalom's my lover
A physical feeling or how my belly's
Empty of Absalom my son
A sequence of falling
Stars and a sword striking
The magnet on its heart
A precise feeling:
What makes you struggle
And what brings you rest
The wind
Where does the wind
Take you my son.

FROM *TWO GARDENS* (1969)

Preannual Poem

Apropos Godard

It's been suggested there's another sex.
It's good to know that someone knows about it.
If there is another sex, br
ing it here so that we might know it, let's sp
eak frankly, is there or isn't there.
Since by now we're sotired of our wi
ves and our virginal girlfriends and all
the while they show us pictures of th
is other thing and we too fe
el there must be something to it.
And if there is another sex in some other
world new women who know how why do
n't they bring a few here to te
ach our worn out women and may
be they'll also throw open the borders wh
en we're tired and can'tbr
eathe.

Two Gardens

If raisins grew on you from head to toe
I'd pluck them off one by one with my teeth and leave your smooth
White body naked and you'd be naked, how hard it is
To feel naked. But there's something disgusting about this sight
So I say: the greenery here is not repulsive
The greenery here is undulant and sweet, plants of paradise.
Cheery tall-built birds so unlike
People, have you called me unprepared

To look at an animal? Still beset by disgust before curiosity
I think, oh it's nothing limbs it's nothing my blood
And later I run to see only animals so unlike
People. There are no thorns. Everything's soft and lovely.
There are no pits. We're in an eternal garden. The fruits are full
Of themselves. This garden will vanish and no plant will grow like
The plants in this singular garden.
I'm afraid. I see a horizon. My body is disappearing and my soul knows
A horizon's drawing near. There are some very common
Repulsive plants, and there are some people, flesh and
Blood and growth of nails and hair. I see
Them. The earth is flat and small. The flesh and blood are thick and
    alive
The colors are like being, strong and forlorn.
And later we're back in the first garden, round and intertwined.
The sweetness of course is neither like honey nor like sugar
The sweetness is of nectar. And you alone are revealed in the leaves.
If we were somewhere else and I'd call you My Lord
You'd see that I'm as smooth as oil. Or a pearl.
But in this meticulous garden I am light and you are a species.

The House Is Empty

The house is empty and the trough is broken
And Naomi my heart's delight where has
she gone? The house lies plundered, the closets
are empty. And Naomi's gone off how frightful
What garments what rags cover her
body. The groves are parched, the earth
abandoned. Wild grasses and nettle.
Donkeys tread the dust no longer
and Naomi strikes them not.
Naomi my heart's delight. A hen
some water and life but Naomi where are you
oh maiden, oh who would not revive her,
if only Naomi could live her life
and there'd yet be joy in our meadows

This Poem Should Have Etc.

A northern light should have been veiled like Venus, with
A lake whose ice seems to melt like honeycomb at noon.
Pliant stems amid the flowery grass and wide-
Leafed hedges enveloping their wooden props.
Every thing should have been wrapped in something.
Young girls' heads in ample northern scarves
A lake in ice, sorrow in ceremony and custom in lore.
Our blazing summer denies such plans.
Elegant graves and air-conditioning are still luxuries
And the season ripens sevenfold after you make off to
An air-conditioned café, where they watch what you're doing and say
Look, mister, this here's no office. It's no illusion
When each season the temperature in the streets
Is fixed by the ballot box, and seasonal feats
Like bits of Byzantine mosaic confirm visions linked
To the climate, if only it were so in my day, such strange hallucinations
Someday they'll be seen as some silly protocol linked
Firmly to date and place. While everyone's frantic about his mobility
Like Hermes, and we dream retrospectively, polishing the butts of his
    pistols
Like Hermes, never moving without his regalia
Like this poem which should have been a northern poem, summer strips
    it bare
Closes off longing for a different light by craving to death another
    century.

Lola

Lola, are you still getting whatever you want
Have you got everything you wanted
Do you still want Lola
Or what happened to you after you got it.

Did you want something new Lola after
So many years and your voice Lola
Do you still want the same voice.
Do they still want you Lola like they used to.

Youth is like a memory Lola, silencing,
And rhymes scatter with an editor's whisper
What will you wear on that day that

You bend over the first fountain betraying all time
Drinking and murmuring pleasure in a voice growing younger by the
    minute.
And vanish with an undying wish into an infant of yourself.

Are These Moods of Mine Memory

Are these moods of mine memory
A bird call wings thin standing
Perfume apple face turning for air
I float in these I'm so perplexed.

And drawing near and just now moving back
A certain coldness before me for things
And when they're festive they cleanse the body
God lives in every thing.

Pain and purity valiant as the living
If only they'd change to dimmer forms
For all this they're forever faithful.

FROM *POETRY* (1976)

Never Will I Hear the Sweet Voice of God

Never will I hear the sweet voice of God
Never will his voice pass beneath my window
Great drops will fall on the open plains a sign
God will not come to my window again
How might I see his sweet body again
To plunge into his eyes I'll never descend to draw forth again
Looks will change in the world like wind
How will I recall this beauty without crying
Days will pass through my life like body convulsions
By fragments of touch memories shattering still more from weeping
The shape of his movement charms the air as he moves
Never will the voice of longing pass beyond the threshold
When he resurrects man like his dead with memories, like being
If only his sweet look would stand by my bed and I'd cry.

At Sea

The place no longer exists
And they're already hunting someone at sea
I've joined with them
But what am I doing to you Tonya
What have I learned here, there? Someone's
Forcing me so many people
Each one said what suits him
Even made a suitable gesture, at sea
It seemed for a moment you deserved it Tonya (the outer I)
Alone at sea
Surrounded by people
Each one does what suits him

What have I turned you into Tonya (the inner I)
They're lowering you into the boat but it won't help you
In the end you're bound
You've grown so much only you are there
There's always doubt
Misjudgment's maintained;
Bound? Beautiful
No background and no people
While you're alone in space and time
On all sides things grow less and less
Whom have we joined with so that things grow less
The sea the people and whoever's victorious over deeds
Your ties to things
This victory at the expense of things that add up by themselves
Sitting alone at sea
And anyhow why have I called you Tonya
We say we wanted to achieve this
You were Tonya we had a grudge against you
And we committed these acts against you
Acts you once committed against us
Because we've learned how to do these things
And we do them
We help
Not for us not against us
But for you, against you, we free them from there
We don't identify ourselves
Still we free them from there
At sea
Cleansing their hands guiding them this once
And it all happens just to Tonya
Who was a huntress of man and came to be bound at sea
Blood wants quiet
Or maybe angels are blood's desire
Just to take Tonya, I, innocent,
A person responsible for creating saints there
For after me they sanctify   they follow me as well
And next time we'll forgive and no more exalt Tonya.

The Body

On him was her soft dead body
And she had some face and some order about her
And she could not have known him since she was dead
And he would not have violated her in any way
And in his hands she seemed contrite
Her insides were dead flowers an expired spring
She was like his land in his hands the delight of his fathers
Once someone else's love object
Perceived to the last as a mixed blessing
He was careful not to learn too much from her death
She was like a mask that has no meaning behind it
Like the worst thing that could happen   the opposite of real
A picture of eventual fate   a lesson that's never begun
She was kept in his hands each moment like death
And he would hold her like complete fullness
A kind of frightening opposite of what could happen to him
Inside himself was a fate overturned
A horror story of reverses that he lived the same
Beauty was left that's the way the gods worked
It's only that in nature nothing was spoiled
One could play with fate as with feeling
Oh go out and play with fate as with feeling
The inside of lamps spoke conclusively
Needles pierced say yes or no
Courteous beasts bore the royal message
Drops came in gushes because of writing
I haven't seen you in years you've become moon-faced
Dying like this is like leaving a note behind

I Feel Empty

I feel empty, empty as a swimming pool,
I told you something a woman doesn't even tell herself,
Then I thought if I were naked,
I tried to reconstruct the beginning, you know
Why it happened, it's awful, I feel empty
Empty as a swimming pool,

What I could have done I couldn't do even from the beginning,
What I could have done before was blotted out, forgetfulness,
It can take days for it to come back, I don't see it,
I'm still not so adept, what a question, coming back
Some response, I'd like to hear from him, you see,
I don't know when I'll have the courage again,
A moment like that comes back, interesting, he's still not on the list
I was helped for a moment, then I changed, is that going back?
I'm waiting, you're silent, like an alter ego, like a second self.

When You're Not a Poet

Lightning flashes soar like rain before your eyes
You're like a dwindling shadow in your face
You move about like a matter before your eyes
Where are you and where's your well-being.
The key is to be something
Then you'll move on differently
Your step is deliberate
And there's something steady upon your eyes.
There's one simple secret
And it's not one of those beyond your life
Be something in this matter
Or they'll devour you as they'll devour your corpse.
From now on it must be so
If there's no soft substance melting before your eyes
If there's nothing solid smashing your face
There is something of you that will enchance your personality(s).
Know who made your life before you
When you don't reveal important secrets
Be something else if you want
But don't let them expel you, from yourself(s).

Gentle as Moon on Water

Gentle as moon on water and not like the cherry tree that said
He will come to me at the hours of upside-down beasts colorless with
    letters among them
                Inscribing my name with no trace of hell
He will do to me whatever I dream, did I hide my head in shame before
    between his knees?
A thing will walk on water for the sake of yearning dreamed up by a
    king
It's not improbable that I'd fling like stones the spinnings in my head
    later
When unfounded frailty begins where would my face go like a river
Ach, not like a beast of prey would be this image a king drew on me in
    his vision
(Or some brutal image that took shape then the soul will recoil from it
    as from a defilement)
What can be sicker here facing me than a decision white as an eyeball
    revolving before the divine spirit
A pack of thoughts preceded like angels counted on a night whose skies
    open when there's no suspicion
Or with a king or with a lover where the structures of memory are
    stable even loyal
What brings a person to be a child or a person child falling from my
    frailty later to self torture
A face blushes with the redness of apples but maybe not all at once
    maybe with the other not at all.

Splitting the Infinite

"I have so many women" he said inside her
The thousand women who peered out of one face
"I have so many women" he screamed inside her ecstatic

"Man is never alone" he said my chronic
Attempter of suicide "There's so much in every
One of us" there's always someone inside yourself

It sounds like a joke to me "There's always
Someone at home" says the paranoid to the schizophrenic
"One?" said the schizophrenic "I am so so many"

"Another presence is a sort of religious sensibility" I quoted
All this at various times by splitting one place into many
"I have so many women" he said inside herself
As infinite personalities began
Sprouting from the void from the inner air like grass after
Rain like vapor from vast waters like drops of
Infinity women as infinite years presences
In places at infinite times
"In order to do this one must be one" said the latter

All The

All the silly threatening things
The huge kitchen sink
In the crystal tower
When the moment is stretched out over a lifetime
Like a stocking on a whore's leg
Holy works history won't recall
All the devil's works as well
Plans plots fabrications
Lovers like cannibals sitting
And listing life's traumas like foods
In a labyrinth dark and tangled as my soul
Holy spirits and demons are set free
Death delicately picks flowers
With the living he fashions eternal bouquets
Like fears in the dark sparkling spiritual
Children who live off me
The wizard locks them in a tower tells them
German tales
On the other side I move by like a bridge
The Messiah a little child passes beneath me
Suddenly there's light children alive

UNCOLLECTED

Love Poem #2

There was no reason whatever for the critique of pure reason to come
   out of the watermelon like a child

As if bursting from his mother's belly out of the watermelon a child
   critique of pure reason putting hand on heart swearing to love me
   forever

And my heart is broken inside me and my sacred heart is broken a child
   coming out of the watermelon kissing my hand and begging for his
   life putting hand on heart swearing devotion forever

(And my heart is a fountain of youth making lovely gentle sounds
   melting and weeping not cold and frozen as unturned snow the
   sounds and joining broken things and probing)

And there was no reason whatever for the critique of our pure sacred
   and enduring love to topple as pure critiques topple to come out of a
   watermelon like a child placing a hand

On his heart swearing eternal love begging for his life kissing my hand
   breaking my broken heart that's broken even without him

God holding my hand in his kissing my hand shedding his tears on his
   cheek and my heart is broken how could I without him

To See Long like El Greco

To see long and pretty and shiny like El Greco
Or to see round and disjointed and unpretty and weak
To see scattered and fat and disjointed and pieces
Or to see whole and everything and together and in color
And to see the unknown as vaporous

Circles all the unknown disappears
To remove from expression any other framework
And to know everything about other expressions
To see narrow and long and pretty like El Greco

How do things really look
How do things look to one who's lost all knowledge
How do things look to one who's gained all knowledge
How do things really look
To see long and narrow like El Greco
To see lovely and lusty and Gothic
Not to think like Allen Ginsberg that it's all delusion
Not to change neurosis into ideology and end in shock

The feeling of possible potential presses
It's only potential it's not real
It's not real since everything's relative
And it's not truth uncertainty
That's absolute the situation that is the coefficient doesn't change
And it's not true that truth is partial
That pain is partial
That suffering is partial
That happiness is incomplete
That wisdom is partial
That stupidity is partial

The retarded one makes horrible faces
The insane one's face is horrible like his son's face
Consciousness is children
How plant-like we are our children seeds
Consciousness is our children
My consciousness is my next child
Growing like a psycho physical plant
A plant is one thing one taste
A person is all tastes all of them all senses
All possibilities
The wise one cautiously turns his eyes inward
The fruits of the Garden of Eden spoil in the insane one's taste
Fear melts or turns solid into pain
Fear cuts through a living body like a real thing
Keeps you busy in your spare time fear is a free inheritance
Becomes a kind of possession fear shows on your face like a living thing
Becomes totally benign its own features in structures of a living thing
– – – – – – – – – – – – – – –

To Live at the Speed of Biography

Disintegrating at low speeds
Those pent-up forces of evil let loose
The forces of evil in matter the forces of evil in spirit
The intellectual activating forces of evil
Every transformation of matter is accomplished by them
Without intermediaries without descending to any imaginary level
Without intermediary that the newspapers love so much
Without hands without women's discrimination without
Those forces which transform something that's not matter into
Matter that's nearly nonexistent except in the world of evil
Those forces that at the speed of biography are released
Biography's tossed aside like a placenta
A person comes out of a placenta and starts doing witchcraft
He separates from it now from biography
Tries to function now without his life outside
Outside himself now he sits in the field praying
Sits in the field like a spirit outside himself outside his body
He'll still enter his body he'll identify himself
With himself even if he doesn't identify he's no child
A child identifies with a parent a hero a person not with himself
He pretends he's shooting everything everyone himself
He mourns himself he envisions his own funeral
Sheds tears like rain maybe not even this
In one of the situations where nothing seems to happen
He doesn't identify with himself he envisions himself
He's outside his body his body looks vulnerable
He watches himself like a stranger maybe a friend
A minute has passed another minute, already? he remembered
From his throat another voice spoke not his someone else's
He's been speaking with someone else's voice for some time
With the voice of another small child he remembered
Places reminded him places didn't make him forget
He forgot himself slowly he regained himself
Accepted himself again this time he'll be careful he won't rush

He'll live at the speed of biography he'll protect
Himself he'll say soothing, coherent things
He'll invent for its sake all sensuous images just as they are
Without lies only pure, elating images
He's vowed all vows and renounced them like a Christian
He'll turn into all the pious people he's always wanted

He'll speak only with his own voice he'll always be himself
He won't accuse he won't judge he'll love strongly and more
He'll be free as when he was born he's lucky he remembers
Others were killed inside themselves at an earlier age
Not he he remembers the moment of dying
He remembers the moment of resurrection and specific moments
He'll do his best under current conditions
Without favors without connections without waiting too long
Without me my life is impossible he said to himself
And this is all a person has asked for, his life.

With letters woven into carpets of life
A letter or code or existential knowledge
That will tell him something something really about him
Something really known about him the dynamism principle of his life
The power principle of his life something really about him
To live faster than the speed of biography
To live slower than the speed of biography
Early on it's still possible to tell it straight
Soon it will all disappear in the darkness be lost in oblivion
Memory loves daylight the senses night

BIBLIOGRAPHY

The names of certain poets may have several spellings. Variants include: Gouri (Guri); Zach (Sach); Ravikovitch (Rabikovitch, Rabikovitz, or Ravikovich); Wollach (Wallach).

Most of the poets appearing in this anthology have written in other genres—novels, journalistic volumes, essays, translations, plays. Only their volumes of poetry are listed here.

Items marked with an asterisk indicate collections from which poems were selected for this volume. Unless otherwise noted, all items were published in Tel Aviv.

Yehuda Amichai
Akhshav Bara'ash [Now in the storm: Poems, 1963–1968].* Jerusalem: Schocken, 1968.
Akhshav Uvayamim haAherim. Likrat, 1955. (Collected in *Shirim 1948–1962*.)
Bagina haTsiburit. Jerusalem: Akhshav, 1958–59. (Partially collected in *Shirim 1948–1962*.)
Bemerhak Shtei Tikvot. Hakibbutz Hameuchad, 1958. (Partially collected in *Shirim 1948–1962*.)
Me'ahoray Kol Ze Mistater Osher Gadol [Behind all this hides great happiness].* Jerusalem: Schocken, 1974.
Shalva Gedola: She'elot Uteshuvot. Jerusalem and Tel Aviv: Schocken, 1980.
She'at haHesed. Jerusalem and Tel Aviv: Schocken, 1982.
Shirim 1948–1962 [Poems 1948–1962].* Jerusalem and Tel Aviv: Schocken, 1962.
Velo Al Menat Lizkor [Not just to remember].* Jerusalem: Schocken, 1971.
haZman [Time].* Jerusalem: Schocken, 1977.

David Avidan
Be'ayot Ishiyot. Arad Publishing, 1957. (Collected in *Mashehu Bishvil Mishehu*.)
Berazim Arufei Sefatayim. Arad Publishing, 1954. (Collected in *Mashehu Bishvil Mishehu*.)
Mashehu Bishvil Mishehu [Something for somebody: Selected poems, 1952–1964].* Jerusalem: Schocken, 1964.
Shirei Ahava Umin. A. Lewin-Epstein—Modan, 1976. (An anthology of previously collected works.)
Shirei Lahats. Alef, 1962. (Collected in *Mashehu Bishvil Mishehu*.)
Shirei Milhama Umeha'a. A. Lewin-Epstein—Modan, 1976. (An anthology of previously collected works.)
Shirim Bilti Efshariyim. haMe'a haShloshim, 1968. (Includes *Personal Report on an LSD Trip*.)
Shirim Ekroniyim. Akhshav-Masada, 1978. (An anthology of previously collected works.)
Shirim Hitsoniyim. Eked, 1970.
Shirim Shimushiyim [Practical poems].* Jerusalem: A. Lewin-Epstein, 1973.

Sikum Beinayim. Jerusalem: Akhshav, 1960. (Collected in *Mashehu Bishvil Mishehu.*)
Tishdorot Milivyan Rigul [Messages from a spy satellite].* A. Lewin-Epstein–Modan, 1978.

Ory Bernstein
Aviv Veshivro. Adi. 1955.
Be'ona Ketsara [In a short season].* Jerusalem: Schocken, 1967.
Be'oto haHeder, Be'oto haOr. Yokhani, 1962.
Emek haShave [Common ground].* Hakibbutz Hameuchad, 1979.
Erev Im Sue [An evening with Sue].* Hakibbutz Hameuchad, 1976.
Im Mavet. Hakibbutz Hameuchad, 1982.
Kulam Ma'asim Bodedim [They're all separate acts: Poems, 1967–1973].* Mif'alim Universita'iyim Lehotsa'a La'or, 1974.

Amir Gilboa
Ayala Eshlah Otakh [Gazelle I send you].* Hakibbutz Hameuchad, 1972.
La'ot. Orha, 1942. (Partially collected in *Sheva Reshuyot.*)
Kehulim Va'adumim [Blues and reds].* Am Oved, 1963.
Ketaf [Balm].* Hakibbutz Hameuchad, 1971.
Ratsiti Likhtov Siftei Yeshenim [I wanted to write the lips of sleepers].* Am Oved, 1968.
Sheva Reshuyot [Seven domains].* Merhavia: Sifriat Poalim, 1949. (Collected in *Kehulim Va'adumim.*)
Shirim Baboker Baboker [Early morning songs].* Hakibbutz Hameuchad, 1953. (Collected in *Kehulim Va'adumim.*)

Haim Gouri
Ad Alot haShahar. Hakibbutz Hameuchad, 1950.
Ad Kav Nesher: 1949–1975. Hakibbutz Hameuchad, 1975.
Ayuma [Terrible].* Hakibbutz Hameuchad, 1979.
Mar'ot Gehazi [Gehazi Visions].* Hakibbutz Hameuchad, 1974.
Pirhei Esh. Tel Aviv and Merhavia: Hakibbutz Ha'artsi/Hashomer Hatsa'ir, 1949. (New ed. Jerusalem: Tarshish, 1961.)
Shirei Hotam. Hakibbutz Hameuchad, 1954.
Shoshanat Ruhot [Compass rose].* Hakibbutz Hameuchad, 1960.
Tenu'a Lemaga [Movement to touch].* Hakibbutz Hameuchad, 1968.

Abba Kovner
Ad-Lo-Or: Poema Partizanit. Merhavia: Hakibbutz Ha'artsi/Hashomer Hatsa'ir, 1947.
Admat haHol. Merhavia: Sifriat Poalim, 1961.
Ahoti Ketana. Merhavia: Sifriat Poalim, 1967.
El [To].* Hakibbutz Hameuchad, 1980.
Hupa Bamidbar [Canopy in the desert].* Merhavia: Sifriat Poalim, 1970.
Lehakat haKetsev Mofi'a Al Har Gerizim [The rhythm band appears on Mount Gerizim].* Merhavia: Sifriat Poalim, 1972.
Mikol haAhavot [Of all my loves].* Merhavia: Sifriat Poalim, 1965.
Perida Mehadarom. Merhavia: Hakibbutz Ha'artsi/Hashomer Hatsa'ir, 1949.
haSefer haKatan [The little book].* Hakibbutz Hameuchad, 1973.
Tatspiyot [Observations].* Sifriat Poalim, 1977.

Dan Pagis
Gilgul [Transformation].* Ramat Gan: Agudat haSofrim/Masada, 1970.
Milim Nirdafot [Double exposure].* Hakibbutz Hameuchad, 1982.
Mo'ah [Brain].* Hakibbutz Hameuchad, 1975.
Shahut Me'uheret [Late stay].* Merhavia: Sifriat Poalim, 1964.
She'on haTsel. Merhavia: Sifriat Poalim, 1959.

Dahlia Ravikovitch
Ahavat Tapu'ah haZahav. Mahbarot Lesifrut, 1958–59.
Horef Kashe [A hard winter].* Dvir, 1964.
Kol Mishbarekha Vegalekha. Hakibbutz Hameuchad, 1972.
haSefer haShlishi [The third book].* A. Lewin-Epstein, 1969.
Tehom Kore [Abyss calls].* Hakibbutz Hameuchad, 1976.

Meir Wieseltier
Davar Optimi, Asiyat Shirim [Something optimistic, the making of poems].* Mif'alim Universita'iyim Lehotsa'a La'or, 1976.
Kah [Take].* Mif'alim Universita'iyim Lehotsa'a La'or, 1973.
Me'a Shirim [One hundred poems].* Gog, 1969.
Motsa El haYam [Exit to the sea].* Hakibbutz Hameuchad, 1981.
Penim Vahuts. Hakibbutz Hameuchad, 1977.
Perek Alef Perek Bet [Chapter A chapter B].* Jerusalem: Akhshav, 1967.

Yona Wollach
Devarim [Things].* Akhshav, 1966. (Collected in *Shira.*)
Or Pere. Eikhut, Sifrei Adam, 1983.
Shira: Shirim Mekubatsim [Poetry: Collected poems].* Mif'alim Universita'iyim Lehotsa'a La'or, 1976.
Shnei Ganim [Two gardens].* Daga, 1968–69. (Collected in *Shira.*)

Natan Zach
Anti-Mehikon [Anti-erasure].* Hakibbutz Hameuchad, 1984.
Bimkom Halom: Mahberet Italkit Rishona. Galeria Masada, 1966.
Kol heHalav Vehadvash. Am Oved, 1966.
Shirim Rishonim. Jerusalem: Hamasah, 1955.
Shirim Shonim [Different poems].* Author's publication, 1960. (2d ed. Alef, 1964; expanded ed. Hakibbutz Hameuchad, 1974.)
Tsefonit Mizrahit [North-by-northeast: Poems, 1967–1978].* Hakibbutz Hameuchad, 1979.

SUGGESTIONS FOR FURTHER READING

Individual Poets

Amichai, Yehuda. *Amen.* Translated by the Author and Ted Hughes. New York: Harper & Row, 1977.
———. *Love Poems.* [Bilingual edition.] New York: Harper & Row, 1981.
———. *Poems.* Translated by Assia Gutmann. New York: Harper & Row, 1968.
———. *Selected Poems.* Translated by Assia Gutmann and Harold Schimmel. London: Penguin Books, 1971.
———. *Time.* New York: Harper & Row, 1979.
———. *Travels of a Latter-Day Benjamin of Tudela.* St. Louis: The Cauldron Press, 1977.
Avidan, David. *Cryptograms from a Telestar: Poems, Transmissions, Documents.* Translated by the Author (with several translations by Karen Alkalay, Robert Goldy, and Dit Dagan). Tel Aviv: Now Publications, 1980.
———. *Megaovertone.* Translated by the Author and Abraham Birman. London and Tel Aviv: The Thirtieth Century Press, 1966.
Gilboa, Amir. *The Light of Lost Suns.* Translated by Shirley Kaufman with Shlomith Rimmon. New York: Persea Books, 1979.
Kovner, Abba. *Canopy in the Desert: Selected Poems.* Translated by Shirley Kaufman. Pittsburgh: University of Pittsburgh Press, 1973.
———. *Selected Poems: Abba Kovner and Nelly Sachs.* Translated by Shirley Kaufman. London: Penguin Books, 1971.
Pagis, Dan. *Poems.* Translated by Stephen Mitchell. Oxford: Carcanet Press, 1972.
———. *Points of Departure.* [Bilingual edition.] Translated by Stephen Mitchell. Philadelphia: Jewish Publication Society of America, 1981.
———. *Selected Poems: T. Carmi and Dan Pagis.* Translated by Stephen Mitchell. London: Penguin Books, 1976.
Ravikovitch, Dahlia. *A Dress of Fire.* Translated by Chana Bloch. London: Menard Press, 1976; rev. ed. New York: Sheep Meadow Press, 1978.
Zach, Nathan. *Against Parting.* Translated by Jon Silkin. Newcastle upon Tyne: Northern House, 1967.
———. *The Static Element.* Translated by Peter Everwine and Shulamit Yasny-Starkman. New York: Atheneum, 1982.

Anthologies

Anderson, Elliott, ed. *Contemporary Israeli Literature.* Philadelphia: The Jewish Publication Society of America, 1977. [Originally *TriQuarterly* (Evanston, Ill.) 39: *Contemporary Israeli Literature* (Spring 1977).]
Birman, Abraham, ed. *An Anthology of Modern Hebrew Poetry.* New York and London: Abelard-Schuman, 1968.
Burnshaw, Stanley, T. Carmi, and Ezra Spicehandler, eds. *The Modern Hebrew Poem Itself.* New York: Holt, Rinehart & Winston, 1965; New York: Schocken Books, 1966.
Carmi, T. *The Penguin Book of Hebrew Verse.* New York: The Viking Press and Penguin Books, 1981.

Flantz, Richard, ed. *P.E.N. Israel 1974: A Selection of Recent Writing in Israel.* Tel Aviv: The Israel P.E.N. Centre, 1974.

Frank, Bernhard, trans. *Modern Hebrew Poetry.* Iowa City: University of Iowa Press, 1980.

Friend, Robert, ed. *Modern Poetry in Translation* (London), no. 22: *Israel.* (Autumn 1974).

Glazer, Myra, ed. *Burning Air and a Clear Mind: Contemporary Israeli Women Poets.* Athens, Ohio: Ohio University Press, 1981.

Mintz, Ruth Finer. *Modern Hebrew Poetry: A Bilingual Anthology.* Berkeley and Los Angeles: University of California Press, 1968.

Moked, Gabriel, ed. *Now: Poems by Yehuda Amichai and David Avidan; Stories by Aharon Appelfeld and Yitzhak Orpaz.* Jerusalem: Akhshav Publishers, 1969.

Penueli, S. Y., and A. Ukhmani, eds. *Anthology of Modern Hebrew Poetry in Two Volumes.* Jerusalem: Institute for the Translation of Hebrew Literature and Israel Universities Press, 1966.

Poetry from Israel: 1970–1980. Special issue (Winter 1983) of *The Literary Review, An International Journal of Contemporary Writing.* Rutherford, N.J.: Fairleigh Dickinson University.

Schwartz, Howard, and Anthony Rudolf, eds. *Voices within the Ark: The Modern Jewish Poets.* New York: Avon Books, 1980.

Silk, Dennis, ed. *Fourteen Israeli Poets: A Selection of Modern Hebrew Poetry.* London: Andre Deutsch, 1976.

Sonntag, Jacob, ed. *New Writing from Israel 1976: Stories, Poems, Essays.* London: Corgi Books, 1976.

Spicehandler, Ezra, and Curtis Arnson, eds. *New Writing in Israel.* Tel Aviv: Sabra Books, 1976; New York: Schocken Books, 1976.

HEBREW SOURCES

[1] Includes *Sheva Reshuyot* and *Shirim Baboker Baboker* poems.

Author, Poem	*Original Hebrew Title*	*Source*
This whole land belongs to me . . .	Li kol ha'arets hazot . . .	*AEO*, p. 10
They'll all get up. . . .	Kulam yakumu. . . .	*AEO*, p. 12
My city mine. . . .	Iri li. . . .	*AEO*, p. 13
To come free to a city . . .	Lavo ḥofshi le'ir . . .	*AEO*, p. 14
I looked outside. . . .	Ra'iti ḥutsa. . . .	*AEO*, p. 15
When I'm by myself . . .	Keshe'ani le'atsmi . . .	*AEO*, p. 23
Back and forth. . . .	Bein ze laze. . . .	*AEO*, p. 24
I guess it will come suddenly. . . .	Ze kenir'e yavo keḥetef. . . .	*AEO*, p. 25
To run a night's distance . . .	Laruts merḥak layla . . .	*AEO*, p. 26
a city defenseless by day . . .	Ir pruza bayom . . .	*AEO*, p. 44
Times stir in me . . .	Zemanim mit'orerim bi . . .	*AEO*, p. 51

Abba Kovner

Of All My Loves	Mikol ha'ahavot	*Mikol haAhavot* (*MH*), p. 5
The Scientists Are Mistaken	Hem to'im hamad'anim	*MH*, pp. 11–12
How Many Poems Were Lost	Kama shirim avdu	*MH*, p. 25
Lord of Dreams	Adon haḥalomot	*MH*, p. 43
The Voice of My White City	Kol iri halevana	*MH*, p. 56
The Hour's Late	haSha'a me'uḥeret	*Ḥupa Bamidbar*, pp. 245–47
Between mountains . . .	Bein harim . . .	*Lehakat haKetsev Mofi'a Al Har Gerizim*, pp. 26–27
Sun-Watchers	Ro'ei shemesh	*Tatspiyot*[2] (*T*), p. 54
Dinosaurs	Dinozaurim	*T*, p. 156
Dimmed Observation	Tatspit medumdemet	*T*, pp. 24–25
Lookout on a Rock on the Heights of Mount Hermon	Tatspit al sela bema'alot haḤermon	*T*, pp. 37–38
I Don't Know if Mount Zion	Eineni yode'a im Har Tsiyon	*T*, pp. 39–40
Vow	Neder	*T*, p. 61
Front Page	Amud haḥadashot	*T*, p. 143
On My Words	Al milay	*T*, p. 179

[2] Includes *haSefer haKatan* poems.

Author, Poem	*Original Hebrew Title*	*Source*
To the Things That Are Immortal	El hadevarim shehem benei almavet	*El* (*E*), pp. 37–38
Poem: Alte Zachen	Poema: Alte zachen	*E*, pp. 59–63
Tashlich	Tashlikh	*E*, pp. 64–65
While at Prayer	Ve'odo bitfila	*Al haMishmar*, September 17, 1982

Haim Gouri

Mistake	Ta'ut	*Shoshanat Ruḥot* (*SR*), p. 9
It seems to me . . .	Nidme li . . .	*SR*, p. 20
His Mother	Imo	*SR*, p. 114
Piyyut for the New Year	Piyyut leRosh Hashana	*SR*, p. 117
Holiday's End	Kets haḥufsha	*Tenu'a Lemaga* (*TL*), p. 9
You're No King	Einkha melekh	*TL*, pp. 10–11
My Samsons	Shimshonay	*TL*, p. 13
Of the Azazmeh Too	Min haAzazme	*TL*, p. 14
Pictures of Jews	Temunot Yehudim	*TL*, pp. 33–34
Silk and Silence	Meshi vasheket	*TL*, p. 51
Piraeus	Piraeus	*TL*, pp. 53–55
Northern Romance	Romantika tsefonit	*TL*, p. 56
Window-Dreaming with SAS	Beḥalon ra'ava shel SAS	*TL*, p. 57
In the Amorite City	Be'ir haEmori	*TL*, p. 72
flame and wood and blackened stones . . .	Esh ve'etsim va'avanim mefuyaḥot . . .	*TL*, p. 75
An Age Is Ended	Tam mo'ed	*TL*, p. 78
And of all that was theirs . . .	Umikol asher lahem . . .	*Mar'ot Geḥazi* (*MG*), p. 35
I live now in an ancient book . . .	Ani gar ka'et . . .	*MG*, p. 53
I'll be an amulet . . .	Ehye kame'a . . .	*MG*, p. 61
I pray you . . .	Ana, silḥu-na . . .	*MG*, p. 67
And This Happened	Veze haya	*Ayuma* (*A*), p. 19
At the Train Station	Betaḥanat harakevet	*A*, p. 20
Album	Albom	*A*, pp. 35–36
Dance	Maḥol	*A*, p. 37
Thorns	Kotsim	*A*, p. 48
Jericho	Yeriḥo	*A*, pp. 53–54
If	Im	*A*, p. 58

Yehuda Amichai

God Has Mercy on Kindergarten Children	Elohim meraḥem al yaldei hagan	*Shirim 1948–1962* (*S*), p. 14
My Father	Avi	*S*, p. 27

Author, Poem	Original Hebrew Title	Source
Look, Thoughts and Dreams	Re'i, mahashavot vahalomot	S, p. 30
Lovers in Fall	Ohavim bastav	S, pp. 40–41
Instructions for the Waitress	Hora'ot lameltsarit	S, pp. 161–62
The Onus of Mercy	Bekhol humrat harahamim	S, p. 219
From "Jerusalem 1967"	Yerushalayim 1967	*Akhshav Bara'ash (AB)*, pp. 9, 10
Quick and Bitter	Mar venimhar	AB, p. 26
In My Time, at Your Place	Bizmani, bimkomekh	AB, p. 27
Patriotic Reflections	Mahshavot le'umiyot	AB, p. 38
I Am a Live Man	Ani adam hay	AB, p. 44
We Will Live Forever	La'ad nihye	AB, pp. 68–69
Elegy	Elegiya	AB, pp. 92–93
Now in the Storm	Akhshav bara'ash	AB, p. 183
Jews in the Land of Israel	Yehudim beErets Yisra'el	*Velo Al Menat Lizkor (VAM)*, pp. 13–14
Testimonies	Eduyot	VAM, pp. 50–51
From "Achziv"	Akhziv	VAM, pp. 135, 138, 139
From "Songs of the Land of Zion Jerusalem"	Shirei Erets Tsiyon Yerushalayim	*Me'ahoray Kol Ze Mistater Osher Gadol (MKZ)*, pp. 8, 28, 29
From "Laments on the War Dead"	Kinot al hametim bamilhama	MKZ, pp. 90–91
Tonight I think again . . .	Be'erev ze, ani hoshev shuv . . .	*haZman (Z)*, p. 3
Evening lies along the horizon . . .	haErev shokhev le'orekh ha'ofek . . .	Z, p. 41
Late in my life . . .	Me'uhar behayay . . .	Z, p. 66

Dan Pagis

Epilogue to Robinson Crusoe	Epilog leRobinson Crusoe	*Shahut Me'uheret (SM)*, p. 7
Honi	Honi	SM, p. 8
Logbook	Yoman hashayit	SM, p. 11
A witness anew . . .	Ed mehadash . . .	SM, p. 15
A Letter	Mikhtav	SM, p. 19
Needless Return	Shiva meyuteret	SM, p. 35
Decline of an Empire	Sheki'at ha'imperiya	SM, p. 43
Ararat	Ararat	SM, p. 44
Plans	Tokhniyot	SM, p. 72
Testimony	Edut	*Gilgul (G)*, p. 24
Another Testimony	Edut aheret	G, p. 25
Pages of an Album	Difduf be'albom	G, p. 58

Author, Poem	*Original Hebrew Title*	*Source*
I Was Before I Was	Kvar hayiti beterem ani	G, p. 64
Final Exam	Beḥinat-hasiyum	G, p. 67
Autobiography	Otobiografia	*Mo'aḥ (M)*, pp. 7–8
The Limits of Physics	Gevulot hafizika	M, pp. 15–16
Armchairs	Kursot	M, p. 46 `
Biped	Du-regel	M, p. 47
November '73	November shiv'im veshalosh	*Milim Nirdafot (MN)*, p. 12
Siege	Matsor	MN, pp. 14–18
Houses	Batim	MN, p. 31
Tropical Greenhouse	haHamama hatropit	MN, p. 43
Photo at the Bridge	Tsilum biktsei hagesher	MN, pp. 56–57
Words	Devarim	MN, p. 65
Outside the Line	Miḥuts lashura	MN, p. 66
The Souvenir	haMazkeret	MN, p. 72
Acrobatics	Akrobatika	MN, p. 74

Natan Zach

How the Days Passed. Who	Eikh ḥalfu hayamim. Mi	*Shirim Shonim (SS)*, pp. 2–3
Max Is Dead	Max met	SS, pp. 20–22
War Confession	Viduy milḥama	SS, pp. 27–28
Harvest Month	Yeraḥ bul	SS, p. 29
Samson's Hair	Et se'aro shel Shimshon	SS, p. 42
The Painter Paints	haTsayar metsayer	SS, p. 44
Give Me What the Tree Has	Ten li ma sheyesh la'ets	SS, p. 54
I Hear Something Falling	Ani shome'a mashehu nofel	SS, p. 55
Like Sand	Kemo ḥol	SS, p. 62
Prologue to a Poem	Petaḥ leshir	SS, p. 97
Death Came for Michael Rockinghorse	haMavet ba el sus ha'ets Mikha'el	SS, pp. 98–100
In the Course of Time	Bimrutsat hashanim	*Tsefonit Mizraḥit (TM)*, pp. 59–60
A Soft Warm Breeze	Mashav ru'aḥ ḥama	TM, p. 103
The Problem	haBe'aya	TM, pp. 159–60
Nameless	Beli shem	*Anti-Meḥikon (AM)*, pp. 9–11
A Poem Too Late	Shir me'uḥar miday	AM, p. 17
Against Sadness	Neged etsev	AM, pp. 24–25

David Avidan

Longterm Hatred	Sin'a arukatvaḥ	*Mashehu Bishvil Mishehu (MBM)*, pp. 30–33

Author, Poem	*Original Hebrew Title*	*Source*
Man of Mystery	Ish mistorin	*TK*, p. 15
Who Art Thou, O Great Mountain	Mi ata har hagadol	*TK*, pp. 22–23
Human Qualities	Tekhunot enoshiyot	*TK*, p. 29
Like Rachel	Kemo Raḥel	*TK*, pp. 30–31
Poem of Explanations	Shir shel hesberim	*TK*, p. 33

Ory Bernstein

In a Park, in Siena, at Twilight	Began, beSiena, ve'et erev	*Be'ona Ketsara (BK)*, pp. 26–27
Nocturnal Journey	Masa leili	*BK*, p. 57
Mene Mene	Mene mene	*BK*, pp. 75–76
Only from Afar	Keshe'ata marḥik	*Kulam Ma'asim Bodedim (KMB)*, p. 17
Don't Count	Velo limnot	*KMB*, p. 28
From "Poems from Mexico"	Shirim miMexico	*KMB*, pp. 31, 32–33, 34–35, 38
Of All the Splendor	Mikol hazohar	*KMB*, p. 63
Her Words from the Corner	Devareha min hapina	*Erev Im Sue (EIS)*, p. 5
What She Didn't Say	Devarim shelo amra	*EIS*, p. 11
Memories of Her Friend Who Died	Zikhronot odot yedidah shemet	*EIS*, p. 13
An Imagined Description of Myself, in Another Scene	Te'ur shel atsmi, kefi she'ala beda'ati, benof aḥer	*EIS*, p. 15
What She Wanted to Be	Ma shebiksha lihyot	*EIS*, p. 19
And Later by Myself	Ve'aḥar kakh, levadi	*EIS*, p. 27
And after a Long While	Ule'aḥar zman she'avar	*EIS*, p. 31
Time to Leave	Zman lehani'aḥ	*Emek haShave (EH)*, p. 10
A Wind, That Comes on Suddenly	Ru'aḥ pit'om	*EH*, p. 11
At Woods' Edge	Biktsei haya'ar	*EH*, p. 23
This Is a Poem of Love	Ze shir shel ahava	*EH*, pp. 27–31
Games	Mishakim	*EH*, p. 37
A Season when Nothing's in Place	Be'ov	*EH*, p. 38
All This Is My Time	Kol ze zmani	*EH*, p. 40
More Questions	She'elot nosafot	*EH*, p. 50

Meir Wieseltier

Take a Look at My Rebels	Bo tir'e et hamordim sheli	*Perek Alef Perek Bet (PA)*, pp. 8–10

Author, Poem	Original Hebrew Title	Source
Song of the Last Soldier	Shiro shel halohem ha'aharon	PA, pp. 28–29
Saul Re-enthroned	Sha'ul momlakh bashniya	PA, p. 45
Allenby	Allenby	Me'a Shirim (MS), p. 11
Poetry's Buried	Shira nivla'at	MS, p. 42
Here in Netanya	Kan, biNetanya	MS, p. 72
God's Fire upon Children	Esh Elohim al yeladim	MS, p. 88
Take poems, but don't read them.	Kah shirim, ve'al tikra.	Kah (K), p. 5
Too Short	Katsar miday	K, p. 16
On Guard	Al hamishmar	K, p. 26
Note	He'ara	K, p. 35
Leningrad: Picture Postcard	Leningrad: geluyat nof	K, p. 36
Caution Prevents Accidents	Zehirut mona'at te'una	K, p. 88
Site	Atar	Davar Optimi, Asiyat Shirim (DO), p. 13
Everyone passes under the moon . . .	Kol adam over tahat hayare'ah . . .	DO, p. 14
Holy Is the Desire to Proclaim the Existence of God	Kadosh haratson lehakhriz al metsi'ut haEl	DO, p. 31
From "Elegies by the Senses"	Elegiyot al-yad hahushim	DO, pp. 81–82
Columns	Turim	DO, pp. 108–109
Love Poem	Shir ahava	Motsa El haYam (M), pp. 32–33
Extended Sonnet on the Death of Isaac Danziger	Sonneta mu'arekhet bemot Yitshak Danziger	M, p. 37
From "Wintry Dawn"	Shahar horpi	M, p. 74

Yona Wollach

Jonathan	Yonatan	Shira[3] (S), p. 7
Christina	Christina	S, p. 19
Sebastian	Sebastian	S, p. 24
Absalom	Avshalom	S, p. 28
Preannual Poem	Shir kedamshnati	S, p. 79
Two Gardens	Shnei ganim	S, p. 100
The House Is Empty	haBayit reik	S, p. 103

---

[3] Includes *Devarim* and *Shnei Ganim* poems.

Author, Poem	*Original Hebrew Title*	*Source*
This Poem Should Have Etc.	haShir haze haya tsarikh vekho	S, p. 104
Lola	Lola	S, p. 105
Are These Moods of Mine Memory	Ha'im halakhei nefesh ele zikaron	S, p. 110
Never Will I Hear the Sweet Voice of God	Le'olam lo eshma et kolo hamatok shel Elohim	S, p. 133
At Sea	Al hayam	S, pp. 138–39
The Body	haGeviya	S, p. 141
I Feel Empty	Hitrokanti	S, p. 143
When You're Not a Poet	Ka'asher einkha meshorer	S, p. 144
Gentle as Moon on Water	Adin kayare'aḥ al pnei mayim	S, p. 149
Splitting the Infinite	Pitsul ba'einsof	S, p. 172
All The	Kol ha-	S, p. 173
Love Poem #2	Shir ahava mis. 2	*Davar*, September 5, 1975
To See Long like El Greco	Lir'ot arokh kemo El Greco	*Siman Kri'a* 7 (May 1977): 39–40
To Live at the Speed of Biography	Liḥyot bimhirut habiografia	*Siman Kri'a* 7 (May 1977): 41–42

INDEX